Confessions of a Textbook Writer

If you promise not to get too mad, I'll tell you a secret. I used to write textbooks.

Yes, it's true. I helped write those big books that break your back when you carry them and put you to sleep when you read them. But let me say one thing in my own defense: I never meant for them to be boring!

I used to spend long days in the library, searching for stories to make my history textbooks fun to read. And I filled up notebooks with good ones—funny, amazing, inspiring, surprising, and disgusting stories. But as you've probably noticed, textbooks are filled with charts, tables, lists, names, dates, review questions . . . there isn't any room left for the good stuff. In fact, every time I tried to sneak in a cool story, my bosses used to drag me to this dark room in the basement of our building and take turns dropping filing cabinets on my head.

Okay, that's a lie. But they could have fired me, right? And I've got a wife and baby to think about.

So here's what I did: Over the years, I secretly stashed away all the stories I wasn't allowed to use in textbooks. I kept telling myself, "One of these days I'm going to write my own history books! And I'll pack them with all the true stories and real quotes that textbooks never tell you!"

Well, now those books finally exist. If you can find it in your heart to forgive my previous crimes, I hope you'll give this book a chance. Thanks for hearing me out.

TWO MISERABLE PRESIDENTS

TWO MISERABLE PRESIDENTS

Everything Your Schoolbooks Didn't Tell You About the Civil War

by Steve Sheinkin
illustrated by Tim Robinson

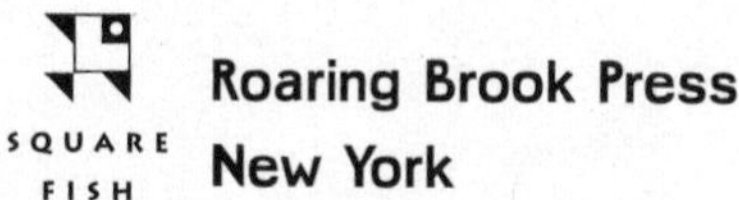

Roaring Brook Press
New York

An Imprint of Macmillan

TWO MISERABLE PRESIDENTS.
 Printed in the United States of America by R. R. Donnelley & Sons Company, Harrisonburg, Virginia. For information, address Square Fish, 175 Fifth Avenue, New York, NY 10010.

Library of Congress Cataloging-in-Publication Data
Sheinkin, Steve.
Two miserable presidents : everything your schoolbooks didn't tell you about the Civil War / Steve Sheinkin; [illustrations by Tim Robinson].
p. cm.
Includes bibliographical references and index.
ISBN 978-1-59643-519-3
1. United States—History—Civil War, 1861–1865—Miscellanea—Juvenile literature. 2. United States—History—Civil War, 1861–1865—Anecdotes—Juvenile literature. 3. United States—History—Civil War, 1861–1865—Biography—Juvenile literature. I. Robinson, Tim, 1963- ill. II. Title.
E468.9.S545 2008 973.7—dc22 2007033115

Originally published in the United States by Roaring Brook Press
First Square Fish Edition: March 2012
Square Fish logo designed by Filomena Tuosto
Jacket and interior design by YAY! Design
mackids.com

10 9 8

AR: 7.0 / LEXILE: 920L

For Anna, in the hope she'll grow up to be a fellow history fan.

-S.S.

Contents

How to Rip a Country Apart

On May 22, 1856, a congressman from South Carolina walked into the Senate chamber, looking for trouble. With a cane in his hand, Preston Brooks scanned the nearly empty room and spotted the man he wanted: Senator Charles Sumner of Massachusetts. Sumner was sitting at a desk, writing letters, unaware he had a visitor. He became aware a moment later, when he looked up from his papers just in time to see Preston Brooks's metal-tipped cane rising high above his head.

Stop That Cane!

So Preston Brooks's metal-tipped cane is about to land on a senator's head. Interesting. But before that cane actually crashes onto Charles Sumner's skull, let's step back and take a look at the events leading up to this moment. Because, believe it or not, if you can figure out why Preston Brooks was so eager to attack Charles Sumner, you'll understand the forces that ripped the United States apart and led to the Civil War.

Mr. Brooks, please hold that cane in the air for just a few minutes. We're going to run through a quick thirteen-step guide to tearing a country in two.

Step 1: Plant Cotton

After finishing college in 1792, a young man from Massachusetts named Eli Whitney headed south in search of a teaching job. He wasn't too interested in teaching, though—he really wanted to be an inventor.

Whitney got his big chance when he met Catherine Greene, who owned a plantation in Georgia. Greene told Whitney that plantation owners wanted to grow more cotton. The problem was, cotton had to be cleaned by hand and it took forever to pick the sticky green seeds out of the fluffy white cotton. If only there was a way to clean cotton more quickly, planters could grow and sell much more of it.

Greene set up a workshop for Whitney, and he quickly came up with an invention he called the cotton gin ("gin" was short for engine). Whitney proudly announced the benefits of using his machine: "One man will clean ten times as much cotton as he can in any other way before known and also clean it much better."

Before Whitney's invention, farmers grew cotton only along the Atlantic coast. Now they raced to plant more cotton, forming a wide belt of cotton plantations across the southern United States, from the Atlantic Ocean all the way west to Louisiana and Texas. Plantation owners made huge profits selling their cotton to clothing factories in the northern United States and in Great Britain. Cotton became so valuable to the economy that Southerners declared: "Cotton is King!"

This was great for Southern plantation owners and Northern factory owners. But it was terrible for enslaved African Americans. Planting and picking cotton took huge amounts of work, and that work was done by slaves. So as plantation owners planted more and more cotton, they decided that they needed more and more slaves. The number of people enslaved in the South jumped from just over 1 million in 1820 to about 4 million by 1860.

Step 2: Grow Apart

At the same time, the states of the North gradually ended slavery. This was partly because many Northerners thought slavery was wrong. But let's be honest: it was mainly because slavery just didn't make sense in the Northern economy. Most farmers owned small family farms, so they couldn't afford slaves. And factory owners had no interest in owning their workers—they made more money by hiring workers and paying them a few cents an hour.

Slavery was only one of many differences between the North and South in the first half of the 1800s. Most Americans still lived and worked on farms in both the North and South. But life in the North was changing as more and more people moved to cities and took jobs in factories. Immigrants from Europe were also settling in growing northern cities. Northerners were busy building canals and railroads to connect cities and farms. There was less change in the South, where more than ninety percent of the people lived on farms or in small towns. The Southern economy was based on farm products: sugar, rice, tobacco, and especially "king" cotton.

The North and South were developing different ways of life—so what? These differences mattered because they made it harder for Northerners and Southerners to agree on plans for the future. For example, take the issue of tariffs, or taxes on imported goods. Sounds pretty boring, right? But tariffs got people excited in those days. Suppose you asked a Northern factory owner and a Southern plantation owner: "Do you support a tariff on manufactured goods imported from Europe?"

"Of course!" the factory owner might say. "Tariffs make imported goods more expensive. So Americans are more likely to buy things made here in our own factories. And that's good for American companies."

"No way!" the plantation owner might say. "We want to buy the goods we need at the best possible prices. Why should we pay higher prices for manufactured goods just to help make Northern factory owners richer?"

Step 3: Keep Your Balance

Now that the North and South are growing apart, let's look at another issue that's about to cause trouble: land. To put the problem simply: What's going to happen with all that land west of the Mississippi River?

As you probably know, the United States started out as thirteen states along the coast of the Atlantic Ocean. But the country had grown quickly:

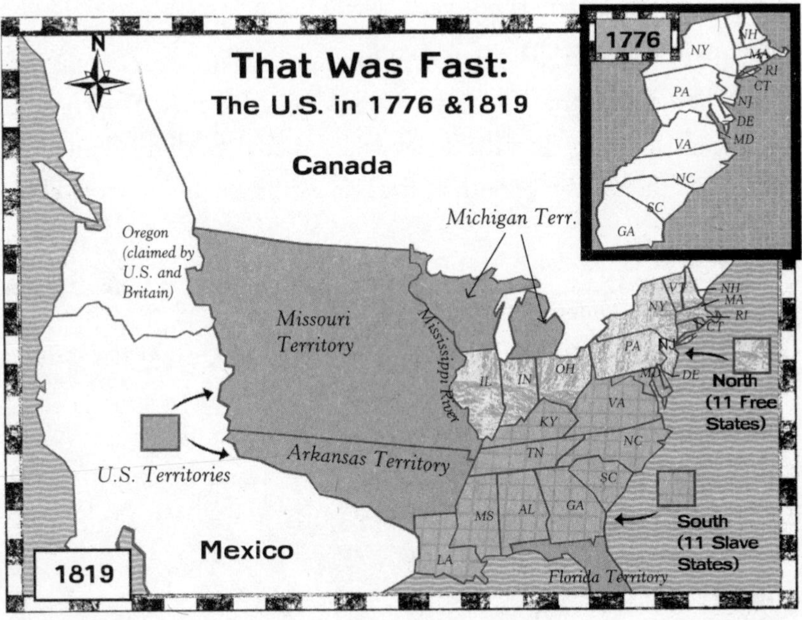

Why is this new land important to our story?

In 1819 there were a total of twenty-two states: eleven "slave states," or states with slavery, and eleven "free states," or states where slavery was illegal. Most members of Congress thought it was a good idea to keep this balance between free and slave states. That way neither North nor South would get too much power in government (or get too angry at the other side).

But everyone knew that western territories would soon be divided up into states—would those new states allow slavery? That was the question Northerners and Southerners were beginning to argue about.

So when Missouri asked to join the Union as a slave state, Congress worked out a deal called the Missouri Compromise. In 1820 Missouri joined the Union as a slave state. And to keep the balance, Maine joined as a free state.

What about all the land west of Missouri? Members of Congress drew a line west from the southern border of Missouri. They agreed that the territory north of the line would someday be divided into free states, and the territory south of the line would be divided into slave states.

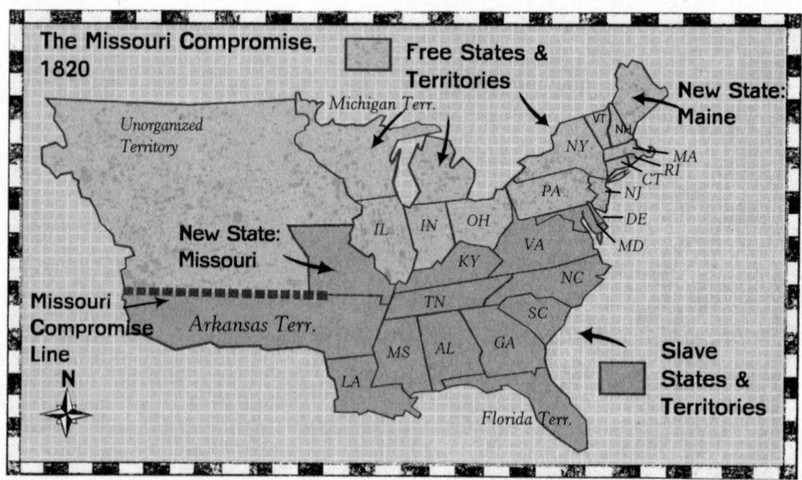

The goal was to protect the balance between North and South. Think it worked?

Step 4: Fight Slavery

Frederick Douglass was not interested in keeping the balance. Born into slavery in Maryland, Douglass grew up working on farms—and thinking nonstop about slavery. How could one person own another? "Why am I a slave?" he wondered. "I will run away. I will not stand it."

When Douglass was eighteen, the man who owned him put him to work in a Baltimore shipyard. One day four white workers attacked him with bricks, knocking him down and kicking him in the face over and over. Fifty white men just stood there watching. Douglass's owner ("Master Hugh," as Frederick called him) went to a judge to complain:

> Judge Watson: *Who saw this assault of which you speak?*
> Master Hugh: *It was done, sir, in the presence of a shipyard full of hands.*
> Judge Watson: *Sir, I am sorry, but I cannot move in this matter, except upon the oath of white witnesses.*
> Master Hugh: *But here's the boy; look at his head and face, they show what has been done.*

But Douglass was a slave, a person with no rights. His word meant nothing. The white workers who had seen the beating refused to testify, so the men who had attacked Douglass were never punished.

Douglass continued working (and giving every cent he earned to Master Hugh). And he thought more and more about trying to escape to the North. He knew the danger. If caught, he could be sold to a cotton plantation far to the south.

He came up with a simple, daring plan. In the South, free African Americans had to carry "free papers"—identification papers proving they were not slaves. Douglass borrowed these papers from a free friend who was a sailor. Then he dressed in sailor's clothes, put the borrowed papers in his pocket, and boldly walked onto a train. The train started north through Maryland.

There was only one problem: free papers included a description of the person, and Douglass looked nothing like his friend.

Douglass tried to quiet his pounding heart as the conductor came through the black passengers' car inspecting everyone's papers. "This moment of time was one of the most anxious I ever experienced," he later wrote.

"Had the conductor looked closely at the paper, he could not have failed to discover that it called for a very different looking person from myself, and in that case it would have been his duty to arrest me on the instant, and send me back to Baltimore."

Frederick Douglass

But the conductor only glanced at the papers, then handed them back to Douglass. The train sped north, and that afternoon Douglass reached the free state of Pennsylvania. He continued on to New York. "I found myself in the big city of New York," he remembered, "a free man."

Douglass soon found work in a Massachusetts shipyard. And he became an active abolitionist—part of a movement to end slavery in the United States.

Step 5: Build a Railroad

Frederick Douglass found another way to battle slavery. He used his house as part of the Underground Railroad, a secret system of routes used by people escaping from slavery. Houses like Douglass's were known as "stations"—places where runaway slaves could rest and hide during the day. Daring "conductors," both black and white, guided escaping slaves from station to station all the way to Canada, where slavery was illegal.

The most famous Underground Railroad conductor was a five-foot-tall woman named Harriet Tubman. Tubman grew up enslaved in Maryland, suffering beatings and whippings that left permanent scars on her body. In 1849, when she was twenty-nine, she found out she was about to be sold. She set off on a hundred-mile walk to freedom, helped along by Underground Railroad conductors who guided her to Pennsylvania.

"When I found I had crossed that line, I looked at my hands to see if I was the same person," she said. "I was free, but there was no one to welcome me to the land of freedom." She was thinking of her family—they were all still living in slavery.

"I was free, and they should be free." Tubman said. "I would make a home in the North and bring them there."

Tubman spent the next ten years planning and carrying out at least thirteen rescue missions, guiding about three hundred people to freedom. Can you guess why she liked to operate in winter? The nights were longer in winter, and it was safer to travel in darkness. Safer not only for escaping slaves, but for Tubman too. Angry slave owners were offering a $40,000 reward for her capture.

Only a small minority of Northerners were abolitionists or Underground Railroad conductors. But their work was causing growing anger in the South. Slave owners saw it like this: *Slavery is perfectly legal in the South, and we have invested our money in slaves. Slaves are our legal property. These abolitionists are trying to steal our property. They're trying to make us poor! How would they like it if we came up north and took away their farms and factories?*

You might answer: *But you have no right to own slaves in the first place!* But for now we're not talking about right and wrong. We're just trying to figure out how Northerners and Southerners got angry enough at each other to rip the country in two.

Step 6: Get More Land

Speaking of getting angry, the North and South soon had something else to fight over—more land. By 1848 the United States looked like this:

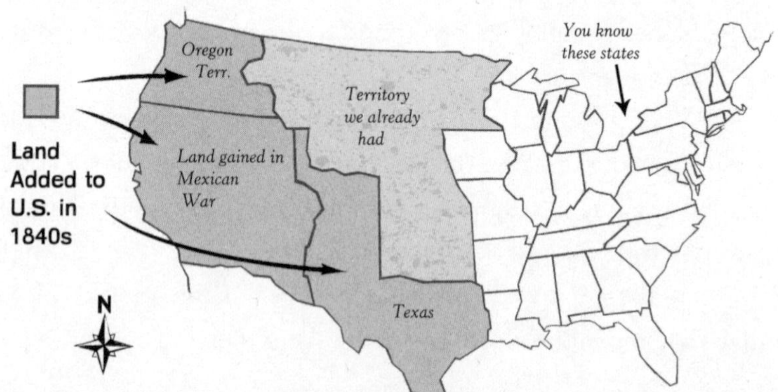

Then gold was discovered in California and thousands of miners raced west, dreaming of quick riches. Suddenly California had enough people to become a state—and it wanted to enter the Union as a free state.

At this time there were thirty states: fifteen free states and fifteen slave states. Was California going to upset this careful balance? Not if Southern leaders could help it. Senator Jefferson Davis of Mississippi summed up Southern fears: "For the first time, we are about to permanently destroy the balance of power between the sections."

Some Southern members of Congress began to talk openly of "disunion"—the breakup of the United States.

Step 7: Try to Compromise

H*old on,* said Senator Henry Clay of Kentucky, *we can work this out.* Clay offered a compromise designed to keep the peace between North and South. The two most important points were these:

By 1850, though, a lot of people didn't feel like compromising anymore. Senator John C. Calhoun from South Carolina declared that the Union could be saved only if the North met Southern demands: stop helping escaped slaves, stop the abolitionist movement, and promise to keep the balance between free states and slave states. He was too sick to give a long speech (he actually died a month later), but he sat in the Senate chamber, a blanket over his legs, while a fellow senator read his emotional words: "The South asks for justice, simple justice, and less she ought not to take."

Senator William Seward of New York rejected Calhoun's demands. Slavery was going to end whether Calhoun liked it or not, Seward insisted. And there was no way he was going to allow slavery to spread into California or any other new territory. "I cannot consent to introduce slavery into any part of this continent which is now exempt from what seems to me so great an evil," Seward said.

This was all part of a months-long argument that included a few fistfights on the floor of Congress. At one point Senator Henry Foote of Mississippi actually pulled out a pistol and aimed it at Missouri senator Thomas Hart Benton.

"I have no pistols!" Benton shouted. "Let him fire! Stand out of the way and let the assassin fire!"

Foote didn't fire.

In the end, most members of Congress agreed with Senator Daniel Webster of Massachusetts. Webster spoke passionately in favor of keeping the peace between North and South:

Daniel Webster

"I wish to speak today, not as a Massachusetts man, nor as a Northern man, but as an American . . . I speak today for the preservation of the Union."

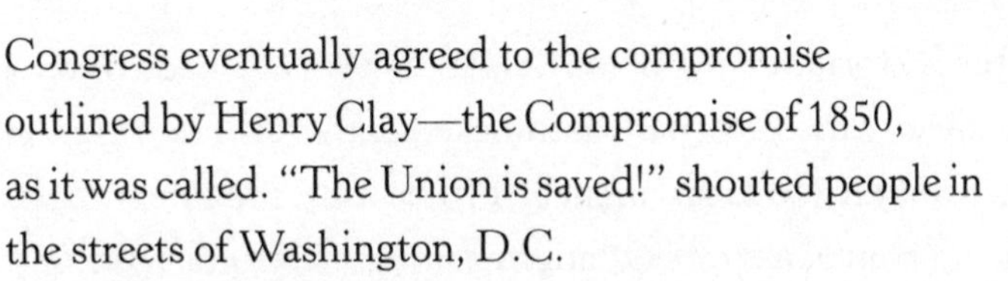

Congress eventually agreed to the compromise outlined by Henry Clay—the Compromise of 1850, as it was called. "The Union is saved!" shouted people in the streets of Washington, D.C.

Unfortunately for the Union, the Compromise of 1850 made people madder than ever.

Step 8: Chase Fugitives

According to the tough new Fugitive Slave Act, any African American suspected of being a fugitive slave could be captured and dragged before a judge. The accused person had no right to testify, and no right to a trial by jury. The judge simply decided if this person was really a runaway slave. The judge got five dollars if he set the person free, and ten dollars if he sent the person into slavery!

Many Northerners, even if they had not been abolitionists before, howled in anger at what they saw as a cruel and unjust law. And escaped slaves living in the North knew they were in serious danger. Just ask Henry Brown.

A year before, Brown had escaped from slavery by packing himself into a small wooden crate in Richmond, Virginia, and instructing his friends to mail him to an abolitionist office in Philadelphia. The friends wrote "This side up, with care" on the crate. But the people handling the box didn't pay much attention, and Brown spent several miserable hours upside down. After a twenty-six-hour train ride, Brown, dying of heat and thirst, heard people prying open the box. He had no way of knowing where he was. So as the top of the crate was lifted, it was with tremendous joy that he looked up and saw four fairly confused Philadelphia abolitionists staring down at him. Brown stood up and reached out his hand and said, "Good morning, gentlemen."

Soon after passage of the Fugitive Slave Act, Henry Brown (now famous as Henry "Box" Brown) was attacked and nearly captured in Providence, Rhode Island. He managed to beat up the kidnappers, but he knew he could be grabbed at any moment. He got on a ship and sailed to Britain.

Step 9: Write Books

Henry Brown was lucky—most fugitives didn't have rich friends to buy them tickets to Europe. Slave catchers stalked the streets of Northern cities, kidnapping escaped slaves and sometimes even African Americans born free in the North.

A writer named Harriet Beecher Stowe was so mad, she had to do something. But what? Her sister-in-law gave her an idea: "Hattie, if I could use a pen as you can, I would write something that will make this whole nation feel what an accursed thing slavery is."

Stowe began writing a book, working at night (after putting her six children to bed) at the kitchen table in her family's house in Maine.

In her novel, which she called *Uncle Tom's Cabin,* Stowe tried to make readers feel the horrors of slavery. She forced parents to imagine what it would be like to see a slave trader coming to buy their only child.

Harriet Beecher Stowe

"If it were your Harry, mother, or your Willie, that were going to be torn from you by a brutal trader, tomorrow morning,—if you had seen the man, and heard that the papers were signed and delivered, and you had only from twelve o'clock till morning to make good your escape,—how fast could you walk? How many miles could you make in those few brief hours . . . ?"

Published in 1852, *Uncle Tom's Cabin* broke readers' hearts, inspiring many in the North to hate slavery like never before. Offended Southern writers fired back with books of their own, arguing that slaves in the South were actually well treated and happy. They insisted that Northern factory workers were much worse off than enslaved African Americans.

Step 10: Divide Nebraska

With tensions between North and South reaching new heights, we now turn back to the most explosive issue: what to do with all that western land?

Senator Stephen Douglas of Illinois thought it was time to divide the huge Nebraska Territory into smaller territories that could become states. But there was a problem. All this land was north of the line drawn in the Missouri Compromise (see Step 3), so it could only be made into free states. Southern senators would never allow this, Douglas knew.

Douglas proposed a solution: We'll throw out the Missouri Compromise and make a new deal called the Kansas-Nebraska Act. We'll divide the territory in two: Nebraska in the north and Kansas in the south. And we'll let the people who settle in the territories vote on whether or not they want slavery.

Congress passed the Kansas-Nebraska Act in 1854, and President Franklin Pierce signed it into law.

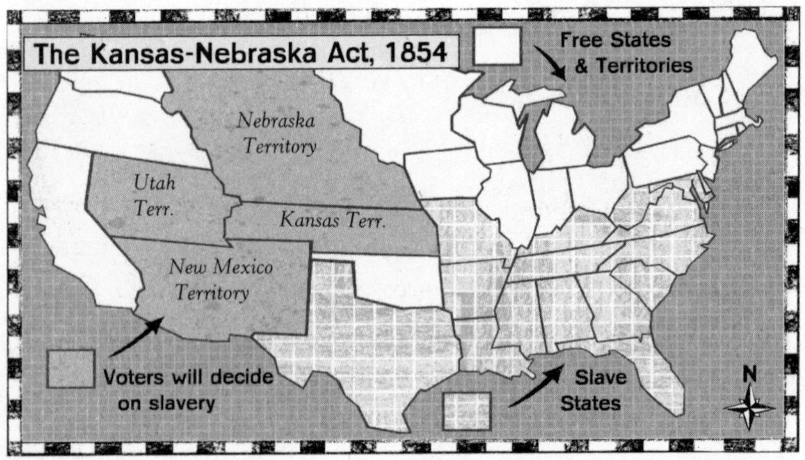

Douglas really thought this would stop the North and South from fighting over slavery in the territories. After all, now it was up to the settlers themselves to decide the slavery question. That was democracy, right? Self-government? Who could be against that?

Actually, lots of people. When Douglas went home to give a speech in Chicago, an angry crowd shouted at him for two solid hours, finally driving him off the stage. In Peoria, Illinois, people were calm enough to listen to Douglas's defense of the Kansas-Nebraska Act. Then a lawyer and former member of Congress named Abraham Lincoln rose to respond. Lincoln was so tall and skinny, people said it looked as if he unfolded as he stood up.

Lincoln launched his attack based on one simple idea: "There can be no moral right in connection with one man's making a slave of another." Slavery was wrong, he argued, and they should not allow it to spread to new territories. Did white people really have the right to vote on whether or not they could own black people? Was this really self-government?

"When the white man governs himself, that is self-government; but when he governs himself, and also governs another man, that is more than self-government—that is despotism."*

But whether Lincoln liked it or not, the people of Kansas were going to vote on the slavery question. Which side would win? That would depend on who got there first.

* *tyranny*

Abraham Lincoln

Step 11: Race to Kansas

Supporters and opponents of slavery set off on a race to Kansas. New England abolitionist groups sent money and guns to anti-slavery settlers. But the pro-slavery side had an advantage: the slave state of Missouri was right next to Kansas. The Missouri senator David Atchison took a vacation from Congress to personally lead Missouri men into Kansas. "There are eleven hundred men coming over from Platte County [Missouri] to vote," he said, "and if that ain't enough we can send five thousand—enough to kill every *#$%! abolitionist in the Territory."

And sure enough, just as Kansas was about to elect its first government, five thousand Missouri men rode in and voted—illegally, since only real residents of Kansas were supposed to vote. The new legislature quickly legalized slavery in Kansas.

Calling this government "the bogus legislature," anti-slavery settlers held their own election. The anti-slavery settlers, also known as "Free-Soilers," chose their own government, and, of course, banned slavery. So by the beginning of 1856, Kansas had two different governments meeting in two different cities. Both sides were storing up weapons and organizing armies.

Luckily, that winter was bitterly cold, with temperatures dropping to twenty-nine degrees below zero. Most people stayed inside.

But by May it was warm enough to fight. An eight-hundred-man pro-slavery army marched to Lawrence, home of the Free-Soilers' government. The invading army chased out the Free-Soil leaders, dumped two newspaper printing presses into the Kansas River, and fired a cannon at the Free State Hotel.

The hands of Northern readers shook with fury as they read the next day's newspapers. "STARTLING NEWS FROM KANSAS—THE WAR ACTUALLY BEGUN—LAWRENCE IN RUINS—SEVERAL PERSONS SLAUGHTERED," shouted the headlines of the *New York Tribune.* (Actually, no one was slaughtered, though one pro-slavery man died when a chunk of the Free State Hotel fell on his head.)

Step 12: Insult Senators

No one was angrier about events in Kansas than Senator Charles Sumner of Massachusetts. In a speech he called "The Crime Against Kansas," Sumner called the pro-slavery army "murderous robbers from Missouri . . . picked from the drunken spew and vomit." He also slammed senators who supported the Kansas-Nebraska Act, saving his most personal attack for Andrew Butler of South Carolina. Sumner charged Butler with loving slavery—and also hinted that Butler stammered and spat when he talked. This was a low blow, since Butler had difficulty speaking due to a stroke that had left him partially paralyzed. Even Sumner's friends were a bit offended. And Butler's friends were exploding with rage.

That brings us all the way back to the point where we began: with the cane-swinging Congressman Preston Brooks.

Step 13: Hit Him Again!

Preston Brooks was Senator Butler's cousin. Two days after Sumner's speech, Brooks walked into the Senate chamber looking for revenge. He strode up to Sumner's desk and declared: "I have read your speech twice over, carefully. It is libel [a false and harmful statement] on both South Carolina and on Senator Butler, who is a relative of mine."

Then Brooks began beating Sumner on the head with his metal-tipped cane. Blood flowed down Sumner's face as he tried to wriggle his long legs out from under his desk, which was screwed into the floor. Sumner finally ripped up the desk, along with some of the floor, then stumbled to the ground. Brooks continued smacking Sumner until his cane snapped and he was yanked away by other members of Congress.

Brooks was thrilled to find that his attack on Sumner made him a hero in the South. "Every Southern man is delighted," he boasted.

One Virginia newspaper commented: "The only regret we feel is that Mr. Brooks did not employ a horsewhip . . . instead of a cane." Dozens of Southerners sent him new canes, some with cute sayings on them such as "Hit Him Again!"

Northerners were stunned by this reaction. One member of Congress had beaten another nearly to death and was considered a hero!

Now you know why Brooks attacked Sumner—and you can see that the events leading to this attack were splitting the country apart. The conflict between the North and South was bitter, personal, and a little bit bloody.

It was about to turn seriously violent.

John Brown Lights the Fuse

John Brown was in Kansas to fight slavery. When this emotional abolitionist heard about the attack on Lawrence, he "became considerably excited," witnesses said. And when he learned of the beating of Senator Sumner, he "went crazy—crazy." Brown told his small band of supporters to sharpen their swords and grab revolvers and rifles. They set out after dark, as Brown put it, to "strike terror in the hearts of the pro-slavery people."

Blood Flows in Kansas

John Brown was fifty-six years old, the father of twenty children. He had spent much of his adult life helping slaves to escape—and starting businesses that failed (he was sued twenty-one times, usually for not paying his debts). Now he and his sons were in Kansas, determined to win this land for the cause of freedom.

After the attacks on the town of Lawrence and the head of Sumner, John Brown decided it was up to him to get revenge on proslavery forces in Kansas. "Something must be done to show these barbarians that we too have rights," he said.

"I hope you will act with caution," said a Free-Soil man.

> *"Caution, caution, sir. I am eternally tired of hearing that word caution. It is nothing but the word of cowardice."*
>
> ***John Brown***

On May 24, 1856, just before midnight, John Brown knocked on the door of the cabin of a pro-slavery settler named James Doyle. Behind Brown stood four of his sons and three other men, all with guns and swords.

"What is it?" asked James Doyle from inside the cabin.

Brown said he needed directions to a neighbor's house. But when Doyle opened the door, Brown charged inside, announcing himself as "the Northern Army" and demanding the surrender of Doyle and his family. Doyle's wife, daughter, and three sons jumped out of bed to see what was going on. Brown ordered Doyle and his two older sons, ages twenty and twenty-two, to step outside. He left the rest of the family inside.

Brown's men marched Doyle and his two sons about a hundred yards down the dark road, threw them to the ground, and cut open their heads with swords. Brown and his crew visited other cabins that night, killing two more pro-slavery men and leaving their sliced-up bodies in the dirt.

When the bodies were found the next morning, it was the South's turn to be furious. "WAR! WAR!" declared a Missouri newspaper. A pro-slavery paper in Kansas called the killings an "abolitionist outrage" and demanded immediate revenge.

Pro-slavery forces went on the attack, burning Free-Soilers' cabins, stealing their horses, and searching for John Brown. Free-Soil armies struck back, and all-out war erupted in Kansas—or as newspapers now called it, "Bleeding Kansas."

More than two hundred men were killed in Kansas in 1856. And the issue of slavery was still far from settled.

Dred Scott Denied

Meanwhile, back in Washington, D.C., the Supreme Court was about to give the North and South something else to fight about.

Here are the facts of the case: A black man named Dred Scott was enslaved, owned by a white army surgeon from Missouri, Dr. John Emerson. In the 1830s Emerson had taken Scott with him to a few army bases in Illinois and the Wisconsin Territory—areas where slavery was illegal. In 1846 Scott had sued for his freedom from John Emerson's wife, Irene (John had recently died). Scott told the judge that he had lived for years in a free state and free territory, and therefore he should be free:

"Believing that under this state of fact, that he is entitled to his freedom, he prays your honor to allow him to sue said Irene Emerson in said Court, in order to establish his right to freedom."

Dred Scott

After more than ten years in court, Scott's case reached the United States Supreme Court. Chief Justice Roger B. Taney of Maryland was a proud defender of the South and saw this as his big chance to strike a blow for Southern rights. (Maybe his last chance: he was eighty.)

In 1857 the Supreme Court ruled that Dred Scott was still a slave. Why? Because blacks were not citizens of the United States, wrote Chief Justice Taney, and they had "no rights which the white man was bound to respect." In other words, Scott had no right to bring his case to court in the first place.

But since he had, Taney went on to rule that there should be no free territory, because Congress has no right to ban slavery in territories. Slaves are property, Taney said, and the government cannot tell citizens where they can and cannot take their property.

Southern slave owners cheered that their rights had finally been protected. But opponents of slavery were shocked—and scared too. What next? Would the Supreme Court rule that slavery was legal everywhere in the United States?

Senator Lincoln?

Abraham Lincoln was one of many Northerners upset by the Dred Scott decision. To Lincoln, the Court's decision demonstrated that supporters of slavery had too much power in the national government. He planned to help change that. "I have really got it into my head to try to be United States Senator," he told friends.

His wife, Mary, agreed that Abe could be a senator—she only wished he would act like one. Lincoln had the embarrassing habit of answering their front door in his slippers. And he wore baggy, sloppy clothes, and a tall black hat in which he kept notes and letters. One day some kids knocked off Lincoln's hat and his important papers fell out and scattered all over the sidewalk. As Lincoln calmly bent down to gather the papers, the laughing kids jumped onto his back.

That was Lincoln—he just wasn't a fancy guy. Born in a tiny log cabin in Kentucky in 1809, Lincoln had spent only about a year in school. He made up for this by reading every book he could get his hands on. He even stuck books in his pockets before going out to the field to plow. As twelve-year-old Abe explained: "The things I want to know are in books. My best friend is the man who'll git me a book I ain't read."

The Lincoln family moved west to Indiana, and then on to Illinois. By the time Abe turned eighteen, he was six feet four inches tall, with long limbs rock hard from years of farmwork. "He can sink an axe deeper into wood than any man I ever saw," a friend said. He was also unbeatable at wrestling. When he was twenty-three, Lincoln decided to run for the Illinois state legislature. He traveled around Sangamon County talking to voters (and wrestling many of them). On Election Day he came in eighth.

Lincoln ran again two years later—and won. He was a natural politician, the kind of guy who could walk into a room full of strangers and have everyone cracking up in a few minutes. But he had another side, a quiet and gloomy side. He sometimes sat still for hours, staring silently into the air. "I never saw a more thoughtful face," a friend said of Lincoln. "I never saw so sad a face."

By the time he was fifty Lincoln had served in the state government and the United States House of Representatives, and had become a successful lawyer in Springfield, Illinois. But he had a bigger dream: to return to Washington, D.C., as a U.S. senator. And he got his chance in 1858 when the Republican Party announced: "Abraham Lincoln is the first and only choice of the Republicans of Illinois for the United States Senate."

Who were the Republicans? The answer requires . . .

A Brief Word About Political Parties

At this time there were two main political parties in the United States: Democrats and Republicans. Just like today, Democrats and Republicans fought over all kinds of issues. But it was the issue of slavery in the western territories that caused the bitterest debate.

The new Republican Party had been founded in 1854, and it opposed the expansion of slavery in the western territories. The Republicans got nearly all their support from the North. Members of the Democratic Party argued that slavery should be allowed in the territories if white settlers wanted it. The Democrats had some supporters in the North, but they got most of their support from the South.

Long Abe vs. the Little Giant

Now back to "Long Abe" Lincoln and his 1858 Senate dreams.

The man who had the job that Lincoln wanted was Senator Stephen "the Little Giant" Douglas. Douglas's nickname was based on two things: he was little (just over five feet), and he had the powers of a giant in Congress. Douglas, who was a Democrat, knew Lincoln would be a tough opponent. "You have nominated a very able and a very honest man," he told a Republican friend. "I shall have my hands full."

Lincoln opened the contest with an alarming prediction—the North and South were speeding toward a dangerous showdown: "A house divided against itself cannot stand." Lincoln said. "I believe this government cannot endure permanently half slave and half free. I do not expect the Union to be dissolved—I do not expect the house to fall—but I do expect it will cease to be divided. It will become all one thing, or all the other."

The only way to prevent Northern states from becoming slave states, Lincoln argued, was to stop the expansion of slavery right now.

Douglas thought this was ridiculous, and he said so over and over when the two candidates met in a series of famous debates all over Illinois. Lincoln and Douglas argued for three hours at a time before huge outdoor crowds—crowds that took part in the action by laughing, cheering, and, when they felt like it, yelling out insults and comments. When Lincoln took out a piece of paper to read something aloud, one person shouted, "Put on your specs!"

"Yes, sir, I am obliged to do so," Lincoln said, putting on his glasses. "I am no longer a young man."

This got a big laugh.

Newspaper writers followed the Lincoln-Douglas debates, printing the arguments for the entire country to read. Lincoln and Douglas, both great debaters, were battling over the very issues that were splitting the country apart.

Douglas attacked Lincoln's idea that the Union could not remain half slave and half free. Why couldn't it? Douglas demanded.

"Let each state mind its own business and let its neighbors alone! . . . If we will stand by that principle, then Mr. Lincoln will find that this republic can exist forever divided into free and slave states."

Stephen Douglas

The obvious solution, Douglas argued, was to let voters in the western territories decide for themselves whether or not they wanted slavery. And everyone else should just butt out.

This was exactly what Lincoln refused to do. Lincoln was not an abolitionist, but he was convinced slavery was evil. "If slavery is not wrong, nothing is wrong," he said. And he was not willing to compromise on what he saw as a simple question of right and wrong.

"That is the real issue. That is the issue that will continue in this country when these poor tongues of Judge Douglas and myself shall be silent. It is the eternal struggle between these two principles—right and wrong."

Abraham Lincoln

By the day of the election both men were exhausted. Trying not to get his hopes up, Lincoln kept telling himself he would never win. But his wife disagreed. "Mary insists," he told a friend, "that I am going to be Senator, and President of the United States, too." Lincoln laughed at this idea. "Just think of such a sucker as me as president!"

Well, Abe was right—this time. Douglas won the election in a very close vote. Lincoln said he was too sad to laugh, too old to cry. "I now sink out of view, and shall be forgotten."

The Return of John Brown

But Lincoln was not forgotten. Mostly because the issues he talked about were becoming more and more explosive.

This was thanks largely to John Brown. Brown somehow made it out of Kansas alive and showed up in New England, where he began raising money for a new plan. Convinced that he had been chosen by God to strike a deadly blow against slavery, Brown now attempted to spark a massive slave rebellion. On the cold, drizzly night of October 16, 1859, Brown marched into the town of Harpers Ferry, Virginia, with an "army" of twenty-one men, white and black.

One of Brown's soldiers was Dangerfield Newby, a former slave who was hoping to free his wife from slavery in Virginia. In his pocket Newby carried a letter from her:

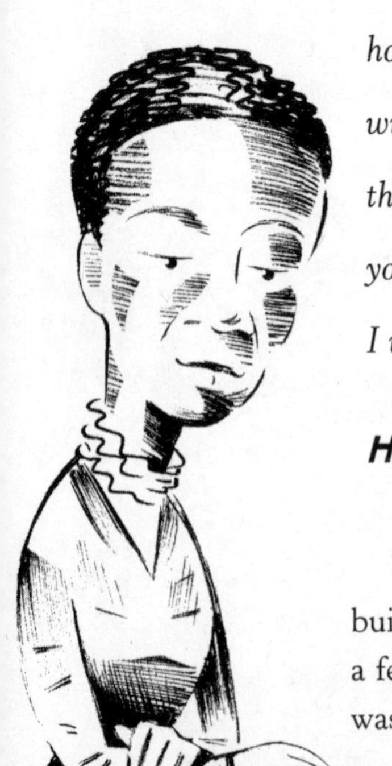

"Dear Husband . . . There has been one bright hope to cheer me in all my troubles, that is to be with you, for if I thought I should never see you, this earth would have no charms for me. Do all you can for me, which I have no doubt you will. I want to see you so much."

Harriet Newby

Brown's small force seized the federal armory—a building full of guns and ammunition. They snatched a few people to hold hostage. (One of the hostages was George Washington's great-grandnephew.)

Then they waited for slaves to race to Harpers Ferry, take the weapons, and start freeing people all through the South.

Ever since that night, people have been arguing about whether or not John Brown was insane. One thing we can all agree on: his plan was very bad. Brown brought no food along and had to send out to a nearby hotel for breakfast for his men and hostages. More important, he didn't arrange any way of letting slaves on nearby farms know what was going on in Harpers Ferry—so how were they supposed to know to join the rebellion?

The people in Harpers Ferry knew what was going on, of course, and they grabbed their guns and began shooting at Brown's army. The first of Brown's men to die was Dangerfield Newby. Within twenty-four hours, a U.S. Army officer named Robert E. Lee led a group of soldiers to Harpers Ferry and attacked Brown's crew. One of Lee's men captured Brown after smacking him on the head with a sword.

Seventeen men lay dead, including ten of Brown's men (two of the dead were his sons). While Brown lay on a cot with his head wrapped in bloody bandages, he was angrily questioned by the Virginia senator James Mason:

Mason: *What was your object in coming?*
Brown: *We came to free the slaves.*
Mason: *How do you justify your acts?*
Brown: *I think, my friend, you are guilty of a great wrong against God and humanity.*

Virginia authorities quickly put Brown on trial, found him guilty, and hanged him on the morning of December 2. He left behind a brief note: "I John Brown am now quite certain that the crimes of this guilty land will never be purged away, but with Blood."

John Brown died knowing he had shoved the nation toward a major crisis. It was as if he had lit the fuse on a massive bomb.

No More Compromise!

As Brown's body swung from the end of a rope in Virginia, church bells tolled in many Northern towns. Cannons fired salutes to Brown's memory. And abolitionist newspapers praised Brown as a hero, even a saint, who had bravely died battling the evil of slavery.

Many Northern leaders, including Abraham Lincoln, spoke out against John Brown's raid. Lincoln considered Brown a madman and a murderer. But this hardly calmed the fury that was sweeping though the South. Southern leaders charged that people such as Lincoln, people who kept hammering away on the slavery issue—they were the ones who had inspired John Brown in the first place.

Nothing terrified white Southerners like the thought of millions of enslaved people, armed and angry, rising in rebellion. And they believed abolitionists and Republicans were working to make this happen. Senator Jefferson Davis of Mississippi accused Northerners of trying "to incite slaves to murder helpless women and children."

Most white Southerners were not slave owners. And most were strong supporters of the Union. But Brown's action was seen as a Northern invasion of the South—practically a declaration of war. "THE DAY OF COMPROMISE IS PASSED" declared a South Carolina newspaper. Southerners naturally sided with their own section of the country. "Never before, since the Declaration of Independence, has the South been more unified," wrote one reporter.

Tensions between North and South exploded in Washington, D.C., where members of Congress showed up to work with weapons tucked into their pants.

"The only persons who do not have a revolver and a knife are those who have two revolvers," said Senator James Hammond of South Carolina. An all-out firefight nearly erupted on the floor of Congress when, in the middle of a furious shouting match, a pistol fell from the pocket of a New York congressman.

What would happen if the country tried to elect a new president at a time like this? Americans were about to find out.

Fire-Eaters Scorch the Little Giant

In April 1860 leaders of the Democratic Party met in Charleston, South Carolina, to choose their candidate for president. After years of leadership in the Democratic Party, Stephen Douglas was pretty sure he would win the nomination. He was in for a shock.

The convention hall in Charleston was filled with "fire-eaters"—Southern Democrats who were no longer interested in compromise with the North. The fire-eaters rejected Stephen Douglas's idea that voters in western territories should vote on slavery. They demanded new laws protecting slavery in all the western territories, and they wanted them now! Fire-eater William Yancy of Alabama spoke to a roaring crowd:

> *"What right of yours, gentlemen of the North, have we of the South ever invaded? . . . Ours is the property invaded . . . ours is the peace that is to be destroyed; ours is the property that is to be destroyed; ours is the honor at stake!"*

William Yancy

Refusing to support Douglas, the fire-eaters walked out of the convention. The Democratic Party split in two—and went on to nominate two different candidates for president: Stephen Douglas in the North and John Breckinridge in the South.

Alexander Stephens, a Georgia leader who hoped to save the Union, feared this split would lead to disaster.

"What do you think of matters now?" a friend asked Stephens.

"Think of them!" Stephens cried. "Why, that men will be cutting one another's throats in a little while. We shall, in less than twelve months, be in a civil war, and one of the bloodiest in the history of the world."

Stephens knew that the votes of Democrats would now be split between two candidates. That would make it much easier for a Republican to win the election. And many Southerners were openly vowing that they would sooner break up the Union than live under a Republican president.

Meanwhile, in Chicago . . .

But Republicans were pretty excited about living under a Republican president. They knew this was their big chance.

The city of Chicago turned into one huge carnival when Republicans met in May to pick their presidential candidate. Liquor flowed at nonstop parties, brass bands played, and everyone marched around waving hats and canes. But they also had some serious business: picking the person with the best chance of winning this election. Republican leaders agreed on a few things:

- We need someone who is respected as honest and intelligent.
- We want someone a little famous, but not too famous. Famous politicians usually have lots of powerful enemies.

• We know we can win the Northeastern states no matter whom we nominate. We need someone who can also win key Midwestern states such as Indiana and Illinois.

The more they thought about it, the more Republicans liked the idea of that tall guy from Illinois, the one who had spoken so well in those debates with Stephen Douglas . . . Abraham Lincoln!

This is just what Lincoln was hoping would happen. He sent a team of friends to Chicago to fight for his nomination. (Candidates never campaigned for themselves in those days—it was considered ungentlemanly.) Lincoln's men worked behind the scenes convincing important Republicans that "Honest Abe" was the most likely man to win a national election. They also found the loudest shouters in Illinois, brought them to the convention hall, and paid them to yell like crazy for Lincoln every time they were given a secret signal. "A herd of buffaloes or lions could not have made a more tremendous roaring," said one reporter.

Back home in Springfield, Lincoln was nervously checking in at the telegraph office every few hours. On May 18 he tried to relax by playing a few games of handball. Then he went with friends to a newspaper office to wait for news. A huge crowd gathered, eager for updates. Finally, an editor ran in with a telegram from Chicago. Lincoln read it to himself, then read it out loud. He was the Republican nominee for president of the United States.

Suddenly swarmed with cheering supporters, Lincoln worked his way through the crowd, telling people, "Well, gentlemen, there is a short woman who will be interested in this news, and I will go home and tell her."

And he went home to tell Mary.

A Four-Way Race to Ruin

The election of 1860 really turned into two different elections—one in the North and one in the South. In the North, Abraham Lincoln battled Stephen Douglas for votes. Lincoln supporters formed "Wide Awake" clubs, groups that marched all night carrying torches, playing horns, and singing their theme song:

Ain't you glad you joined the Republicans?
Joined the Republicans,
Joined the Republicans,
Ain't you glad you joined the Republicans
Down in Illinois?

In the South everyone knew that most of the votes would go to John Breckinridge, or to a fourth candidate, John Bell of Tennessee.

Americans felt a growing nervousness as Election Day approached. Some Southern newspapers were predicting that a Lincoln victory would mean death to the Union. One South Carolina paper put it simply: If Lincoln wins, it said, "there will have to be a separation from the North."

November 6, 1860, was a warm and sunny day in Springfield, Illinois. That

afternoon Lincoln walked over to the county courthouse to vote. Later, after the polls had closed, he walked to the telegraph office and sat down on a couch.

At about nine o'clock the telegraph machines began ticking—news was coming in.

Abe Lincoln's Troublesome Victory

Mary Chesnut was on a train in South Carolina. It was the day after the election of 1860, and everyone was dying to know who had won.

Mary's brother tapped her on the shoulder and said, "Lincoln's elected."

"How do you know?" she asked.

"The man over there has a telegram," he said.

Suddenly the train was filled with talking and shouting, with anger and declarations of Southern pride. Mary Chesnut began keeping a detailed journal—she knew she was about to witness history.

The Trouble with Lincoln

When he found out he had been elected president of the United States, Abraham Lincoln calmly walked home from the telegraph office and told his wife, "Mary, we're elected." The streets of Springfield were filled with cheers and music, but Lincoln didn't feel much like celebrating. He was about to face the most difficult presidency in American history. And he knew it.

The election results help explain Lincoln's worries:

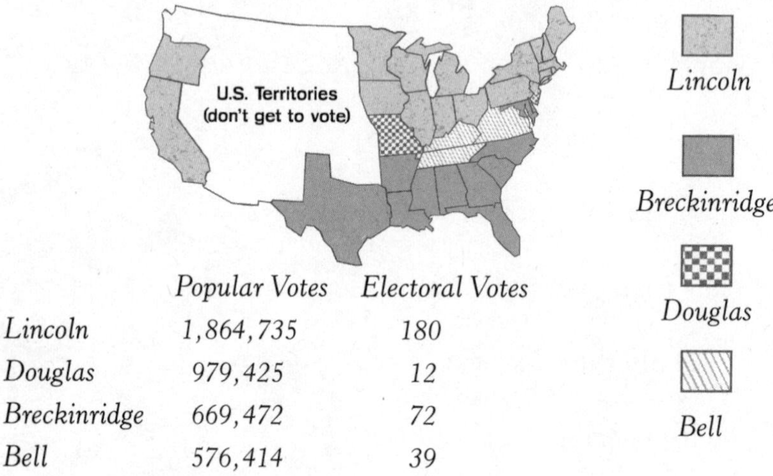

	Popular Votes	*Electoral Votes*
Lincoln	*1,864,735*	*180*
Douglas	*979,425*	*12*
Breckinridge	*669,472*	*72*
Bell	*576,414*	*39*

As you can see on the map, Lincoln got all his support from the North and West. He did not win a single Southern state. In fact, in ten Southern states Lincoln did not even get a single vote!

White Southerners saw their worst fears coming true. They knew that the North's population was growing more quickly than the South's. And now they knew that the North could elect a president without any support from Southern voters. Leaders of several Southern states began talking about seceding, or officially withdrawing, from the United States. One Georgia man saw it like this: "We are either slaves in the Union or free men out of it."

How would you like to be president at a moment like this?

The Last President?

The man who had the job, James Buchanan, couldn't wait to go home. Buchanan still had four months to go until Lincoln took over. Pretty sure the country wouldn't last that long, he often cried out:

"I am the last president of the United States!"

James Buchanan

Buchanan had good reason to worry. On December 20, South Carolina seceded from the United States. Six more states quickly followed: Mississippi, Florida, Alabama, Georgia, Louisiana, and Texas. Leaders from these seven states met in Montgomery, Alabama, to form their own government and write their own constitution. They decided to call themselves the Confederate States of America.

Davis Is Disappointed

On February 10, 1861, Jefferson Davis and his wife, Varina, were cutting roses in the garden of their Mississippi plantation. Jefferson Davis was expecting big news—and dreading it.

When Mississippi seceded from the Union, Davis had resigned from the United States Senate and traveled home. Now he was trying to enjoy a few quiet days on his Mississippi plantation. This was a man badly in need of a vacation. He was exhausted from years in politics. And he suffered from a nerve disease that caused unbearable headaches, making it feel as if the bones of his face were grinding together.

But Davis knew that the new Confederate government was meeting in Alabama. And he suspected they might give him a very important job—maybe commander of the army, or possibly even president. "I would prefer not to have either place," he said.

So Jefferson was worried when a messenger rode up with a telegram. And his face twisted with pain as he read the words. Varina thought someone in the family had died, until he read her the telegram:

> *"Sir: We are directed to inform you that you are this day unanimously elected President of the Provisional Government of the Confederate States of America, and to request you to come to Montgomery immediately."*

Varina said her husband spoke of the news "as a man might speak of a sentence of death." Davis had been chosen, though, and he intended to do the job. "I will do my best," he told her. Huge crowds cheered Davis's train as he traveled to Montgomery. He went to work in an office with "The President" written on a piece of paper and tacked onto the door.

"The South is determined to maintain her position," Davis declared, "and make all who oppose her smell Southern powder." Gunpowder, that is. Peace was still possible—on one condition. "All we ask is to be let alone," Davis said.

But was there really any chance that the Confederate states would be "let alone"? Would the United States government allow seven states to simply break away from the country without a fight?

What do you say, Mr. Lincoln?

A Long Way to Washington

Lincoln couldn't answer this question yet. He was still in Springfield, helplessly watching the country fall apart. He spent his days surrounded by an endless stream of visitors. Some came to meet him or interview him. Some came to ask for high-paying government jobs. Lincoln said his face hurt from smiling so much. "I am sick of office-holding already," he said, long before actually taking office.

It was during this tense and annoying time that Lincoln made a major change in his appearance. Before the election, an eleven-year-old girl from Westfield, New York, named Grace Bedell had written to Lincoln, saying, "My father is going to vote for you, and if I was a man I would vote for you too." She promised to try to convince her brothers to vote for Lincoln—but she felt his chances of winning would be better if he grew a beard. "If you will let your whiskers grow," she wrote, "I will try and get the rest of them to vote for you. You would look a great deal better, for your face is so thin."

Lincoln agreed that his face could use some improvement (actually, he felt he was one of the ugliest men he had ever seen). And he began growing that famous beard that everyone pictures when they think of Abraham Lincoln.

In February the Lincoln family packed up their stuff. Lincoln wrote his new address on each trunk: "A. Lincoln, The White House, Washington, D.C." On the way to Washington, Lincoln stopped to make speeches in dozens of towns—including Westfield, New York. "I have a correspondent in this place," Lincoln told the crowd in Westfield. "If she is present I would like to see her."

"Who is it?" the people shouted. "Give us the name."

"Her name is Grace Bedell," Lincoln said. "She wrote me that she thought I would be better looking if I wore whiskers."

Grace walked up to the stage to meet the next president. Lincoln bent down and said, "You see, I let these whiskers grow for you, Grace." He gave her a kiss, and the people cheered.

The rest of Lincoln's trip to Washington was not as fun. He kept hearing rumors that assassins were going to murder him when he stopped to make a speech in Baltimore. So he decided to skip the Baltimore visit. With a heavily armed friend sitting beside him, Lincoln tried to sleep as his train sped through the night toward Washington. When he arrived at six in the morning, there were no crowds there to greet him—no one knew he was about to show up. He stepped off the train and went to a hotel for breakfast.

Newspapers made fun of Lincoln's arrival, laughing at the idea of a president sneaking into Washington. Cartoons even showed Lincoln traveling in ridiculous disguises—in some drawings he wore clothes borrowed from his wife. Lincoln wasn't even president yet, and he was off to an awful start.

President, Finally

Lincoln finally became president on March 4, 1861. Rumors of a planned assassination were still swirling, so the inauguration ceremony outside the Capitol Building was a bit tense. Everything went fine, though, except for one scary moment when a man fell loudly from a nearby tree. He wasn't up there to shoot anyone, though—he just wanted a good view of the ceremony.

The whole country was eager to hear Lincoln's inaugural speech. Seven Southern states had already left the Union and several more were thinking about seceding.

Lincoln made his opinion clear: individual states did not have the right to secede from the United States. If people were unhappy with recent events in the country, they were free to try to make new laws or even amend the Constitution. But as president, Lincoln said, it was his job to protect the Union. He urged the states that had seceded to come back before it was too late: "In your hands, my dissatisfied fellow-countrymen, and not in mine, is the momentous issue of civil war. The government will not assail you. You can have no conflict, without being yourselves the aggressors."

Lincoln was basically warning the Southern states: Don't do anything you might regret. He didn't talk directly about the crisis brewing at Fort Sumter in South Carolina. But he was thinking about it, and so was everyone else. If there was going to be a civil war, it was probably going to start there. And soon.

Showdown at Fort Sumter

Fort Sumter was a brick fort on a tiny island just off the coast of Charleston, South Carolina. Inside the fort were about eighty United States soldiers, commanded by Major Robert Anderson.

Outside the fort, along the Charleston waterfront, were five thousand Southern volunteers with guns and cannons pointed at Fort Sumter. These men considered the fort to be the property of the Confederate States of America. They wanted it turned over to them—now.

On his first full day as president, Lincoln faced a tricky decision. Anderson and his men in Fort Sumter were running out of food. Lincoln could give up the fort, but that would basically be admitting that South Carolina and the other Confederate states were already independent. He could send in U.S. warships, but that could easily spark shooting, and a huge war.

Any advice for the president?

Lincoln came up with a third option. He announced that he was sending in an unarmed supply ship. It would carry food but no soldiers or weapons. This was clever, because it forced Jefferson Davis to make the next tough decision. Davis could let the food into Fort Sumter, but then Anderson and his men would be there forever. He could blow the ship out of the water, but it would look pretty bad to fire on a ship that was trying to deliver food to hungry soldiers.

Davis sent new orders to General P.G.T. Beauregard, commander of the Confederate forces in Charleston. Beauregard was to demand that Robert Anderson surrender Fort Sumter immediately, before the supply ship had time to arrive. This was a little awkward for Beauregard, who had been a student in Anderson's artillery class at West Point, the U.S. military college. But Beauregard had no choice. He ordered his former teacher to surrender.

Anderson politely refused.

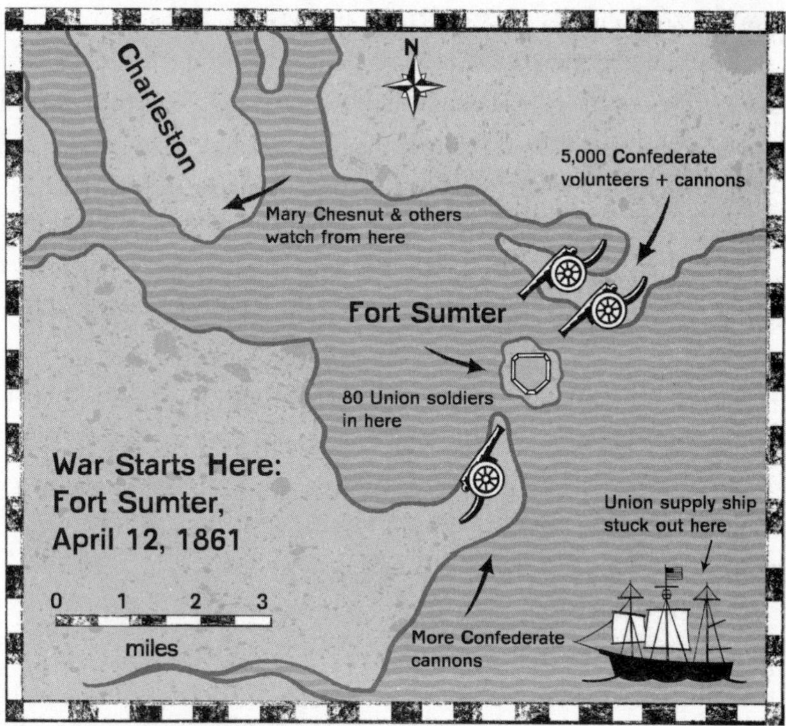

The First Shots

Mary Chesnut was in Charleston, following the story moment by moment. "Why did that green goose Anderson go into Fort Sumter?" she wrote in her diary. "Then everything began to go wrong." Anderson had until four a.m. of April 12 to surrender Fort Sumter. A few hours before this deadline, Chesnut was writing: "I do not pretend to sleep. How can I? If Anderson does not accept terms at four, the orders are he shall be fired upon."

At four thirty that morning, Chesnut heard "the heavy booming of a cannon." She jumped out of bed, said a quick prayer, then ran to the roof of her house and watched the Civil War begin.

Beauregard and his men were blasting forty cannons at Fort

Sumter, streaking the early-morning sky with orange and red. Fires broke out all over the fort, and the men inside began choking on the smoke. "The scene at this time was really terrific," reported Captain Abner Doubleday, who was inside the fort. Soldiers were surrounded by "the roaring and crackling of the flames, the dense masses of whirling smoke, the bursting of the enemy's shells."

Anderson and his men held out for about thirty hours, then surrendered. Amazingly, no one was killed in the fighting. But before leaving the fort, Anderson fired a salute to the American flag—a military tradition. A cannon exploded, accidentally killing Private Daniel Hough. He was the first man to die in the Civil War.

As you will see, almost nothing in this war would go as planned.

Brother Against Brother?

The Fort Sumter news spread quickly across the country. Sixteen-year-old Theodore Upson was working with his father on the family farm in Indiana when a neighbor ran up and said, "The rebs [short for rebels] have fired upon and taken Fort Sumter!"

"Father got white and couldn't say a word," Upson remembered.

That night the family sat around the dinner table, talking about what would happen next.

Grandma: *Oh, my poor children in the South! Now they will suffer!*
Father: *They can come here and stay.*
Grandma: *No, they will not do that. There is their home. There they will stay. Oh, to think that I should have lived to see the day when brother should rise against brother!*

Were brothers really about to fight against brothers? It sure looked like it. People in the North were furious about the Fort Sumter attack. United as never before, they poured into city streets, waving flags and shouting things like "Death to traitors!" One man at a New York City rally declared: "We shall crush out this rebellion as an elephant would trample on a mouse."

Lincoln didn't think it would be quite that easy, but he did hope a strong show of force would help. He called on every state to send soldiers to Washington. He wanted a total of 75,000 troops to serve for ninety days.

Lincoln's call for troops united the South in the same way that the Fort Sumter attack united the North. Southerners were being told to send troops to fight against other Southerners! Not likely! Not only did Southern governors refuse the president's order, but they wrote back nasty letters, such as this one from the governor of Tennessee:

"Tennessee will furnish not a single man for the purpose of coercion, but fifty thousand if necessary for the defense of our rights and those of our Southern brothers."*

Governor Isham Harris

Just two days after his call for troops, Lincoln watched his nightmare come to life—more states started dropping from the Union. Virginia seceded, followed by Arkansas, Tennessee, and

* intimidation

North Carolina. The Confederacy now had eleven states and a new capital city—Richmond, Virginia, just one hundred miles from Washington, D.C.

Both sides raced to get ready for war.

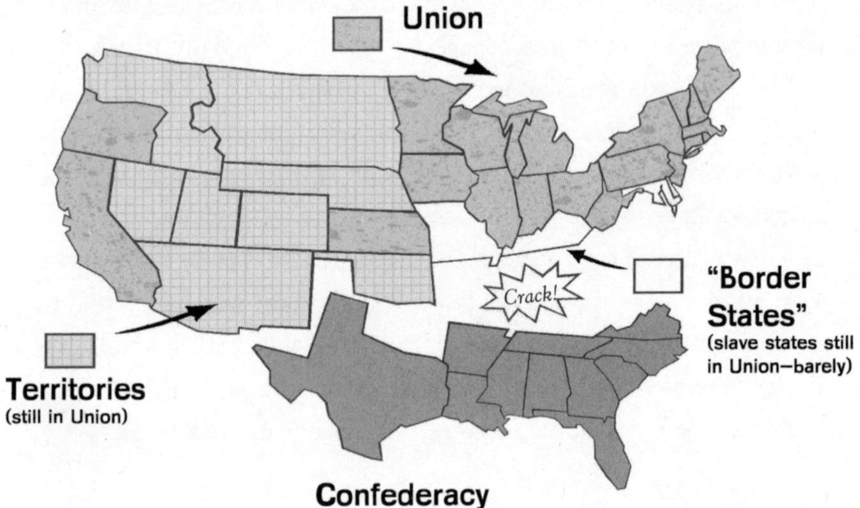

Off to War

Busting with patriotism, thousands of young men rushed to sign up for military service. "So impatient did I become for starting," said one Arkansas man, "I felt like ten thousand pins were pricking me in every part of the body." An Indiana man gave another reason for enlisting: "If a fellow wants to go with a girl now he had better enlist." Everyone on both sides expected this to be a very short war, and they wanted to get in on the action before it was too late.

All over the South volunteers jumped onto trains, then shouted and sang as they rolled toward Richmond. Southern women were excited too—even more excited than the men, according to a young

Georgia woman, who wrote "The women of the South generally were altogether in favor of secession and of the war, if there had to be a war, and if the Southern men had not been willing to go, I reckon they would have been made to go by the women."

"I wish that women could fight," added eighteen-year-old Lucy Breckinridge of Virginia. "I would gladly shoulder my pistol and shoot some Yankees if it were allowable."

The same wave of patriotic excitement swept through Northern towns, where eager volunteers paraded before cheering crowds. As a group of Massachusetts soldiers marched out of town on their way to Washington, family members ran out to give the boys last-minute gifts.

"Our mothers—God bless them!—had brought us something good to eat—pies, cakes, doughnuts, and jellies. . . . Our young ladies, (sisters, of course) brought us . . . needles, pins, thread, buttons, and scissors."

Warren Goss

Warren Goss remembered that one mother actually handed her son an umbrella. Not only was this really embarrassing for the son, but it gives us an idea of how young and inexperienced these men were. Imagine a soldier bringing an umbrella into battle!

Lee Makes His Choice

In an upstairs room in his Virginia home, fifty-four-year-old Colonel Robert E. Lee was pacing back and forth, trying to make up his mind. On the one hand, Lee opposed secession and slavery. And he loved the U.S. Army, in which he had served his entire adult life. On the other hand, he felt he could never fight against his home state of Virginia.

All over the country, people were facing the same question: Are you for the Union or the Confederacy? This question split many families in two, with some family members marching north and others heading south. The Kentucky senator John Crittenden watched one of his sons become a general in the Union army and the other become a general in the Confederate army. And how do you think Abe Lincoln felt when he heard that four of his wife's brothers were fighting for the South!

Even the United States Army was ripped in two. Soldiers who had spent years serving together now had to choose sides in the Civil War. There were plenty of teary farewell scenes as lifelong friends shook hands and hugged . . . then marched off to fight against each other.

Robert E. Lee finally decided to resign from the U.S. Army. He walked downstairs and said sadly to his wife, "Well, Mary, the question is settled. Here is my letter of resignation."

He gave the letter to a very disappointed General Winfield Scott, commander of the U.S. Army. Scott had been hoping Lee would take command of Union forces—he called Lee "the very best soldier I ever saw in the field."

"I could take no part in an invasion of the Southern states," Lee told Scott.

"You have made the greatest mistake of your life," Scott replied. "But I feared it would be so."

Then Lee had to write another difficult letter—this one to his sister, a supporter of the Union. "You must think as kindly of me as you can," he wrote to her.

"With all my devotion to the Union, and the feeling of loyalty and duty of an American citizen, I have not been able to make up my mind to raise my hand against my relatives, my children, my home."

Robert E. Lee

The Confederate government offered Lee command of Virginia's military forces. Lee took the job. On the train to Richmond, he looked out the window and saw crowds of people joyfully celebrating Virginia's secession. This only made him more depressed. It seemed to Lee like the whole country was going crazy.

Now What, Lincoln?

Abraham Lincoln wasn't thrilled with current events either.

From the White House lawn, Lincoln could look across the

Potomac River and see Confederate flags flying in Virginia. A Virginia newspaper boasted that Lincoln lived in constant fear of being captured. "Old Abe has his legs in perfect readiness to run," the paper claimed. "He does not so much as take off his boots."

This was not quite true. The pressure on Lincoln was building, though. Most Union soldiers had volunteered for just ninety days, so Lincoln had to act quickly. Northern newspapers reminded him of this every day, shouting slogans like "Forward to Richmond!" But Lincoln had no idea how to fight a war. He borrowed books on military strategy from the Library of Congress and stayed up late studying them.

General Winfield Scott recommended a blockade of the South—Northern warships would prevent Southern ships from coming or going from Southern ports. This would make it hard for the South to export cotton, or import guns. Lincoln agreed to try the blockade, but he knew it would be years before the North had enough ships to make it really work.

In the meantime, he asked General Irving McDowell to come up with a plan for attacking the Confederate army right away. Known as a pretty good soldier, McDowell was more famous for his massive appetite. After eating an enormous meal, he had once gulped down an entire watermelon for dessert, smacking his lips and declaring the fruit to be "monstrous fine!"

McDowell asked Lincoln for more time, explaining that his soldiers were still "green"—untrained and inexperienced. But Lincoln demanded immediate action. "You are green, it is true," he said. "But they are green also; you are all green alike."

So on July 16, 1861, General McDowell led his untrained army across the Potomac River. They began marching southwest through Virginia.

The Wild Rose of Washington

The Confederate army was ready and waiting—thanks to a spy by the name of Rose O'Neal Greenhow.

Greenhow was a forty-four-year-old widow, a mother of four daughters. As a child in Maryland, she had been known as "Wild Rose." Now she was one of the most popular figures in the busy social scene of Washington, D.C., and was known all over town for her elegance, charm, and humor. She had high-ranking friends in the government and military. They knew she was a strong supporter of the South. But they did not suspect that she was running a spy ring out of her house—just a few blocks from the White House!

Greenhow developed secret codes and put together a team of spies that included store owners, lawyers, her banker, and even her dentist. Through what she called a "reliable source," she learned the details of General McDowell's plans. Then she wrote out a coded message and gave it to one of her secret agents, a young woman named Betty Duvall. Duvall traveled south with Greenhow's message hidden in her long black hair. It read, "McDowell has certainly been ordered to advance on the sixteenth. ROG."

"Yours was received at eight o'clock at night," wrote back a grateful Confederate officer. "Let them come, we are ready for them. We rely upon you for precise information."

Greenhow sent another coded message, this one describing McDowell's attack plans in detail. Confederate generals used this information to prepare an attack of their own.

Picnic at Bull Run

McDowell planned to attack the Confederate army near a creek called Bull Run. But he never expected it would take his army three days to get there.

It was only a thirty-mile march, but McDowell's new soldiers were simply out of shape. They kept stopping to lie down on the side of the road, panting in the harsh July heat. Some ran off to pick blackberries. Others broke into houses along the way, stealing ridiculous things like a giant mirror and a feather bed. A few grabbed piles of underwear and put them on over their uniforms.

Finally, by the early morning of July 21, McDowell had his men ready to attack. The sun began to rise as they marched toward their first battle.

A large crowd of people watched the action from the tops of nearby hills. Hundreds of fancy folks (including sixteen members of Congress) had driven down from Washington, excited to see a real live war. Many even brought picnic lunches. They cheered when they saw the Union soldiers march out into the open field, their metal bayonets sparkling in the morning sunlight. One woman lifted her opera glasses to her eyes and exclaimed about the excitement: "That is splendid! Oh, my! Is not that first-rate? I guess we will be in Richmond this time tomorrow!"

This woman was not alone. On that early morning in July, most Americans believed this was going to be a quick and fairly painless little war.

That was all about to change.

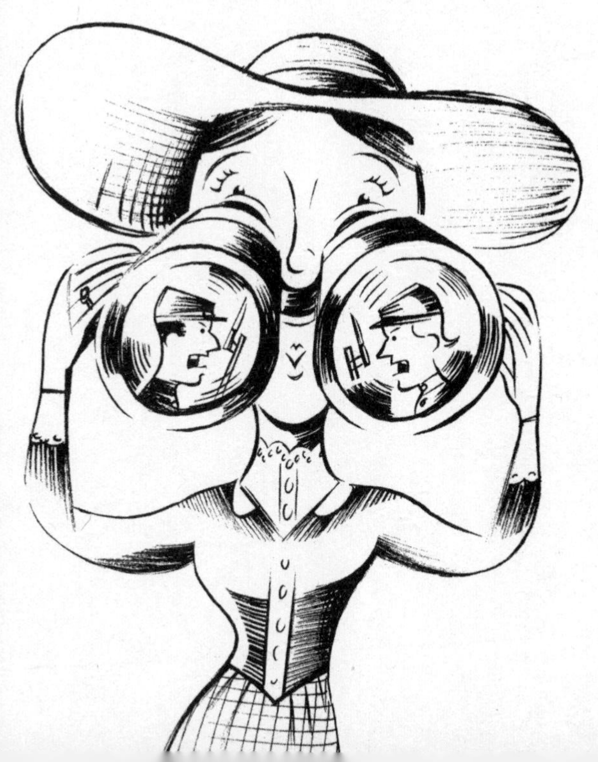

This Is Going to Be Serious

A nineteen-year-old Confederate soldier from Georgia named Berrien Zettler never forgot the night before the first major battle of the Civil War. An officer came to talk to the men, telling them to be ready to attack at daylight. "Remember, boys," he cautioned, "battle and fighting mean death, and probably before sunrise some of us will be dead." Zettler lay down on his blanket. He spent a homesick night beneath the bright summer stars.

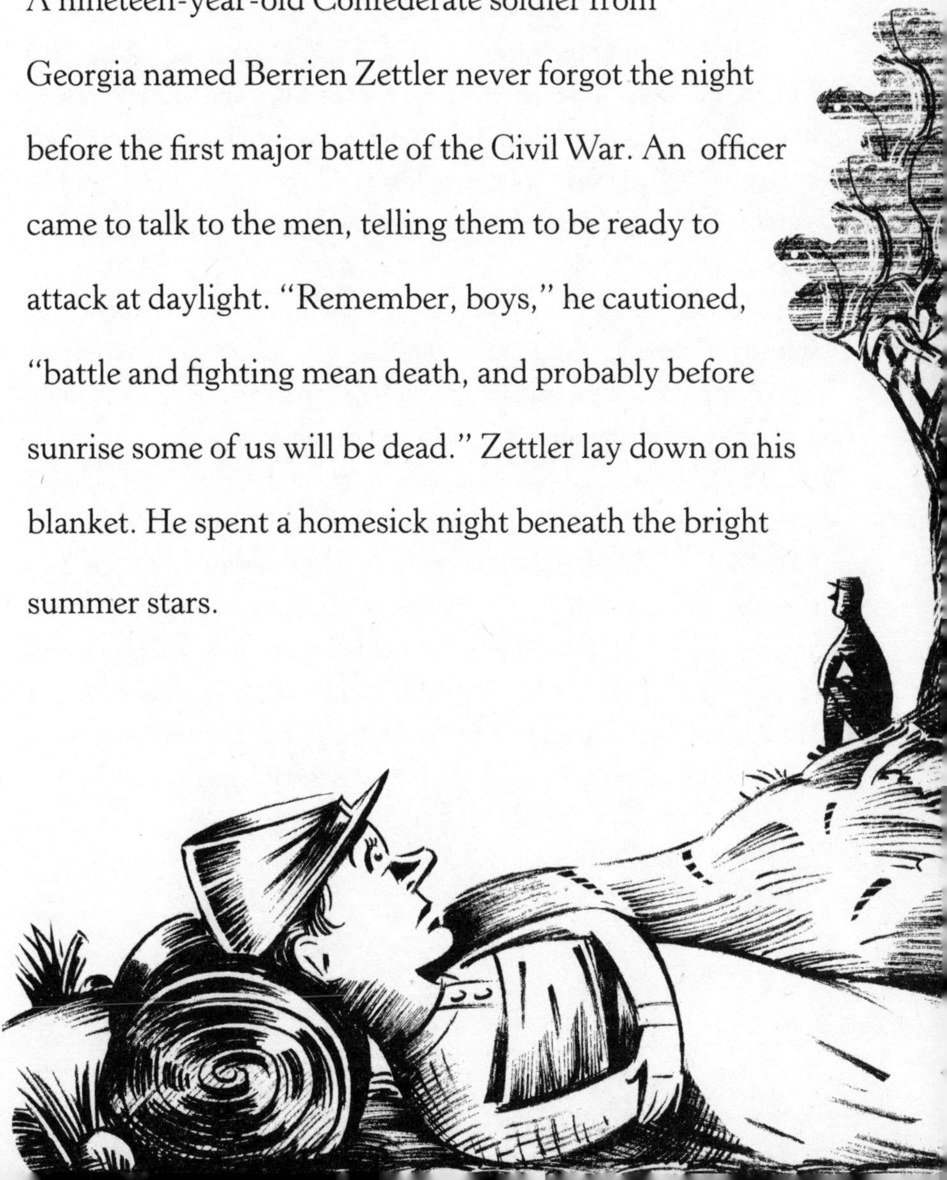

Confusion on the Battlefield

The battle of Bull Run began early the next morning—July 21, 1861. Berrien Zettler's regiment (a group of about seven hundred soldiers) marched through the woods to the edge of a cornfield. They were told to stop, load their guns, and wait for the order to attack the Union forces.

While waiting, the men noticed a big apple tree full of ripe red fruit. Some of them ran to the tree, climbed up, and started tossing down apples. Then a Union bomb came screaming over their heads and exploded nearby. "The boys dropped from the apple tree like shot bears," Zettler remembered. They wriggled on their hands and knees back to their places.

Zettler experienced a rush of terror as he realized the battle was starting. "If my hair at that moment had turned as white as cotton it would not have surprised me," he said. But there was no time to think about it—he charged forward with his regiment.

You'll remember that the Union general, Irving McDowell, planned to attack the Confederate army. But thanks to Rose O'Neal Greenhow, the Confederate general P.G.T. Beauregard knew this, and planned an attack of his own. The result was that two huge, untrained armies stumbled into each other across miles of fields and woods and streams. This was not like a battle in a textbook, where one neat line of soldiers marches toward another neat line of soldiers. This was one enormous, confusing mess. As Berrien Zettler later wrote:

"No one can see a battle, for it covers miles. . . . The excitement is so great that many soldiers do not even see what is going on within a few steps of them."

Berrien Zettler

Zettler kneeled behind a tree, loading and firing as quickly as he could. "But it was impossible to see if my shots hit anyone," he said. Bullets were zooming in all directions and bombs were exploding everywhere. The hot air was filled with smoke and dust. But was anyone actually winning?

The picnickers up on the hills had a pretty good view of the whole thing. And they saw the Northern soldiers slowly driving the Southern troops back. The Union was winning! Members of Congress shook hands and said things like:

"Bravo!"
"Didn't I tell you so?"
"Bully for us!"

Thomas Gets a Nickname

But not all the Southern troops were retreating. The Confederate general Thomas J. Jackson held his soldiers firmly in line. "Steady, men," he told them. "All's well."

This was an encouraging sight to other Confederate troops, some of whom were beginning to panic. General Barnard Bee pointed to Jackson and shouted to his own men:

"Look! There is Jackson standing like a stone wall! Rally behind the Virginians!"

Jackson—soon to be known as Stonewall Jackson—gave his men new orders: they were to wait for the Union soldiers to get close, then fire and charge at the enemy with their bayonets. "And when you charge," he told them, "yell like furies!"

As Jackson's men charged, they let loose a high-pitched shriek that was part anger and part fear. This Southern scream became known as the "rebel yell," and it terrified Northern soldiers in battles throughout the war.

Now the Union army started tripping backwards. Groups of Union soldiers got separated from their commanders and had no idea what they were supposed to be doing. One by one, and then in large groups, Union soldiers started turning from the battle, tossing their guns, and sprinting away.

Up on the hills, the picnickers were getting very nervous. One of them, a newspaper reporter, asked a retreating Union soldier what was happening.

Reporter: *What is the matter, sir? What is this all about?*
Soldier: *Why, it means we are pretty badly whipped, that's the truth.*
Reporter: *Can you tell me where I can find General McDowell?*
Soldier: *No! Nor can anyone else.*

The picnickers jumped into their wagons and whipped their horses and rattled down the hill. They sped onto the road and quickly got tangled up with long lines of shouting soldiers, causing the last thing anyone needed—a terrible traffic jam.

Northerners called this the battle of Bull Run. Southerners called it the battle of Manassas. Either way, 625 Union and 400 Confederate soldiers were killed. It was the bloodiest battle the country had ever seen. And it was nothing compared with what was still to come.

At this point, though, Jefferson Davis felt that the South just about had the war won. "We have taught them a lesson," Davis told the cheering crowds in Richmond.

The scene was very different in Washington, D.C., where exhausted soldiers staggered back into town under a heavy rain, collapsing in the muddy streets. Abraham Lincoln spent a sleepless night on a couch in the White House, listening to the bad news from the battlefield and taking notes on what to do next.

One thing was obvious to Lincoln: defeating the Confederacy was going to be much harder and much bloodier than he had hoped. Lincoln called on the Northern states to deliver 1 million new soldiers. And not for three months this time, but for three years.

Little Mac Takes Command

Lincoln also named a new leader for the Union army: thirty-four-year-old General George McClellan. Thrilled with the opportunity, McClellan wrote to his wife, Ellen:

> *"Who would have thought, when we were married, that I should so soon be called upon to save my country?"*
>
> ***George McClellan***

McClellan got right to work. He spent long days riding around Washington and whipping the army into shape, giving the soldiers a new level of pride and confidence. The men loved him and affectionately nicknamed him "Little Mac" (he was five foot six). "You have no idea how the men brighten up now when I go among them," he told his wife.

The big question was: When was this new and improved army going to march out of Washington and get on with winning the war? Lincoln started urging McClellan to go on the attack. But Little

Mac did not exactly respect the president's military opinions. In fact, he wasn't a Lincoln fan at all. "The president is nothing more than a well-meaning baboon," McClellan said. (He was also known to refer to Lincoln as "the original gorilla.")

One night Lincoln walked to McClellan's house, hoping to have a quick meeting with the general. A servant told Lincoln that McClellan was at a wedding but would be back soon. So Lincoln sat down and waited. About an hour later, McClellan came home and the servant explained that the president was waiting to see him. McClellan shrugged and went upstairs and got into bed. Lincoln sat patiently for another half hour, then asked the servant when McClellan was expected home. McClellan was already home, the servant said—he was upstairs, fast asleep.

Lincoln's advisors considered this a terrible insult. But Lincoln didn't take this kind of thing personally. "I will hold McClellan's horse if he will only bring us success," he said.

Stuck in Washington

Would Little Mac bring Lincoln success? First he would have to actually leave Washington, which he showed no signs of wanting to do. He kept saying his army needed more training. And he became convinced the Confederates had a much bigger army than he did. They didn't.

Another problem was that the spy Rose O'Neal Greenhow was still sneaking intelligence to the Confederate army in Virginia. She regularly got her hands on news from McClellan's meetings, even copies of his notes.

Determined to break up her spy ring, government detectives began watching Greenhow's house day and night. Sometimes the detectives climbed on each other's shoulders to peek in the window. One day, on a street near her house, Greenhow noticed she was being followed. She quickly took a piece of paper from her pocket and ate it, destroying a coded message. The men then hurried up to Greenhow, led by a detective named Allan Pinkerton.

Pinkerton: *You're Mrs. Greenhow?*
Greenhow: *Yes. Who are you? What do you want?*
Pinkerton: *I've come to arrest you.*
Greenhow: *I can't stop you, but if I were in my house I'd have killed one of you before I'd have submitted to this.*

Greenhow was taken to her house and held there under arrest for weeks. Even then, surrounded by guards, she continued sneaking out notes describing McClellan's plans.

By October, McClellan's huge army (which he named the Army of the Potomac) had more than 160,000 men. Still, he wasn't ready to attack. Mac had boldly vowed to "crush the rebels." But now winter was coming and it was clear he wasn't going to do any crushing that year.

Which gives us time to meet two very unusual soldiers.

Two Soldiers: Frank and Harry

Frank Thompson was living in Michigan when the Civil War began. "What can I do?" Thompson wondered. "What part am I to act in this great drama?" Friends marched off to join the Union army. Thompson longed to join them. There was only one difficulty: Frank Thompson was actually a nineteen-year-old woman named Sarah Emma Edmonds.

Two years earlier, Sarah had been living with her family in Canada. One day her father announced that he had picked out a husband for her—a much older man she didn't really like. Sarah dressed up as a man, crossed the border into the United States, and told Americans she was Frank Thompson. Soon she found a job as a traveling book salesman.

In May 1861 "Frank Thompson" enlisted in the Union army. Doctors were supposed to carefully examine all volunteers, but they usually didn't bother. One Union soldier described a typical army "exam."

> Doctor: *You have pretty good health, don't you?*
> Volunteer: *Yes.*
> Doctor: *You look as though you did.*

That was the whole exam. Which explains how Sarah Edmonds became part of the Second Michigan Regiment.

Others members of the Second Michigan looked at Sarah's smooth, hairless face and figured they were seeing a young boy who had lied about his age to get into the army—that was pretty common. Soldiers didn't actually change their clothes very often, which made it easy for Sarah to remain in disguise.

About five hundred women served as soldiers in the Civil War. Some did it for the excitement, others to escape a bad home life. Some joined for the money—the soldier's salary of thirteen dollars a month was much more than young women could earn in jobs that were open to them.

Loreta Janeta Velazquez was one of the women who joined the army in search of adventure. "I was perfectly wild on the subject of war," she remembered. At age nineteen she decided "to enter the Confederate service as a soldier."

Velazquez was living with her husband in Tennessee when the

war started. He quickly set off for Richmond to join the army. "My husband's farewell kisses were scarcely dry upon my lips," she said, "when I made haste to attire myself in one of his suits, and to otherwise disguise myself as a man."

She entered the Confederate army as Harry T. Buford. "This is the kind of fellow we want," said an officer, shaking her hand. "And with a few more of the same sort, we will whip the Yankees inside of ninety days."

Everything went fine for "Lieutenant Buford" until one scary moment at a crowded dinner table. She took a big gulp of buttermilk, soaking her fake mustache. When she tried to wipe the mustache, it started to come off. "To say that I was frightened, scarcely gives an idea of the cold chills that ran down my back," she later said. She described eating the rest of the meal with "my hand up to my mouth all the time . . . doing my best to hold the mustache on."

Velazquez made it through the meal. And a little while later she marched off to war.

Loreta Janeta Velazquez

Attack of the Floating Barn

Meanwhile, Abraham Lincoln was having a rough winter. McClellan was still camped in Washington, still claiming he needed more time to get ready.

In February 1862, Lincoln's eleven-year-old son Willie became ill with typhoid fever. Abraham and Mary watched their son get weaker and weaker and finally die.

"It is hard, hard, hard to have him die!" Lincoln cried at Willie's bedside.

Then, in early March, an alarming report sent Lincoln and his advisors into a panic. A strange new Confederate ship was cruising around Virginia. The ship, Lincoln learned, was once a wooden warship called the *Merrimac*. But the Confederate navy had attached thick sheets of iron to its sides and a long iron beak to its front. They renamed it the *Virginia*. The *Virginia* was so heavy that it had a top speed of just five miles per hour—and it took a half an hour to turn around. Still, it had a huge advantage over the Union's wooden warships.

On the morning of March 8, 1862, several of those Union ships were guarding the mouth of the James River in Virginia, blocking Confederate ships from getting out to sea. It was a warm morning and Union sailors were splashing and swimming in the river. They looked up and saw what appeared to be a giant barn, with just its slanted roof sticking out above the water. This was the *Virginia,* steaming toward the Union ships in a slow-motion charge.

Union sailors scrambled onto their ships and opened fire on the *Virginia.* The men were amazed to see their eighty-pound cannonballs bouncing off their target like "peas from a pop-gun," one sailor said. The *Virginia*'s chief engineer, H. Ashton Ramsey, described the scene. "We were met by a . . . storm of shells. . . . They struck our sloping sides, were deflected upward to burst harmlessly in the air, or rolled down and fell hissing into the water."

The *Virginia* cruised straight at the Union ship *Cumberland.*

"Do you surrender?" shouted the captain of the *Virginia.*

"Never!" the captain of the *Cumberland* replied.

Moments later the *Virginia's* iron beak slammed into the *Cumberland,* cracking a huge hole in the side of the wooden ship. Union sailors jumped off the *Cumberland* as it sank to the bottom of the river. The *Virginia's* iron beak snapped off and sank too.

Even without its beak, the *Virginia* destroyed another Union warship. And before nightfall, three more Union ships got stuck on sandbars while trying to escape the *Virginia's* guns.

The *Virginia* would be back tomorrow to finish the job.

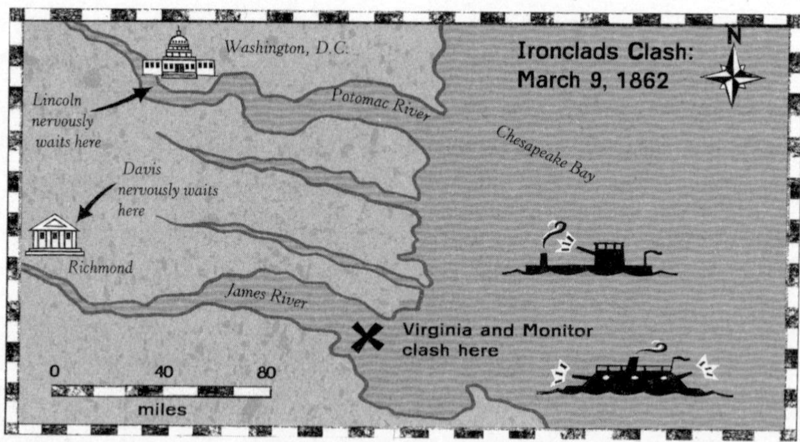

Clash of the Ironclads

When Lincoln heard about all this, he ran to the White House window to see if the *Virginia* was cruising up the Potomac River to destroy Washington.

It wasn't. In fact, the secretary of the navy, Gideon Welles, gave Lincoln some good news: the Union had a new ironclad ship of its own, the *Monitor.* And the *Monitor* was cruising to the James River right at that moment.

The next morning, March 9, the *Virginia* steamed out into the James, ready to finish off the Union warships. Confederate sailors decided to start with the *Minnesota.* But what was that new, weird-looking boat in the river?

"We thought at first it was a raft on which one of the *Minnesota's* boilers was being taken to shore for repairs," said a *Virginia* sailor. Then the raft suddenly starting shooting at them! This was no repair raft—it was the Union ironclad *Monitor.*

For four hours the *Virginia* and *Monitor* blasted their big guns at each other, sometimes from just a few yards apart. Inside the ships, men's eardrums burst and bled from the deafening crash of cannonballs slamming into solid iron. The larger, more powerful *Virginia* tried to ram into the *Monitor*—but it couldn't catch the smaller, quicker Union ship. Though both crews were battered and exhausted, neither ironclad was able to seriously damage the other.

Who won the world's first battle between iron ships? "We of the *Monitor* thought, and still think, that we had gained a great victory," said a Union officer. But the *Virginia* sailors were equally convinced that they had won the day.

Either way, one thing was clear—navies all around the world needed to start building iron ships.

From "Useless" Grant ...

Now the action moves to the west, where there was some good news for Abraham Lincoln. It came from a surprising source: a Union general named Ulysses S. Grant.

Growing up in a small Ohio town, Ulysses was a shy and quiet kid. Bigger kids used to call him "Useless" Grant. And most kids were bigger. At age seventeen, Ulysses stood just five foot one and weighed 117 pounds. He graduated from West Point and fought in the Mexican War, but he was later forced to resign from the army when he began drinking heavily. Then he failed at one job after another. When the Civil War began, Grant was working as a clerk in his father's leather store in Illinois.

He rejoined the army, but no one expected much. Even Grant had doubts about himself. While leading soldiers into one early battle in Missouri, he was so scared, he thought his heart was going to burst through his throat: "I would have given anything then to have been back in Illinois," he said.

Grant marched his men over a hill and looked down at the field where he expected to see a Confederate army led by Colonel Thomas Harris. But Harris and his army had already marched away. Grant was relieved—and he learned a lesson that changed his life:

"It occurred to me at once that Harris had been as much afraid of me as I had been of him. This was a view of the question I had never taken before; but it was one I never forgot afterwards."

After this experience Grant became a completely different kind of military leader. He quit worrying about what his enemy was going to do to him. From then on, he would worry only about what he was going to do to his enemy.

... to "Unconditional Surrender" Grant

In February 1862, Grant led attacks on key Confederate forts on the Cumberland and Tennessee rivers. These rivers were like highways through the South. Whichever side controlled the rivers was able to control the whole region.

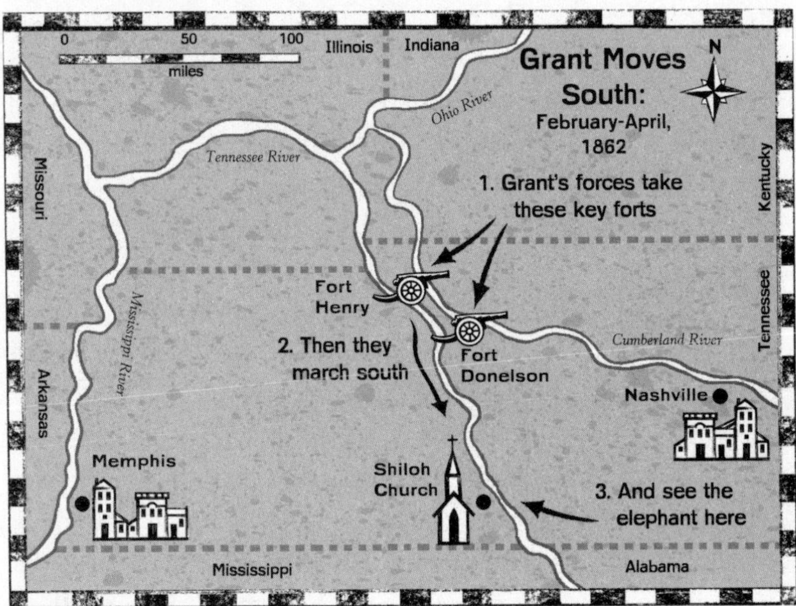

Union forces quickly captured Fort Henry. Then Grant surrounded Fort Donelson, trapping about 15,000 Confederate soldiers inside. The Confederate commander, Simon Buckner, sent a note to Grant saying, basically, *Let's talk this over.*

Grant refused. "No terms except unconditional and immediate surrender can be accepted," he wrote back.

Buckner was pretty offended. He and Grant were old West Point pals, and he had once loaned Grant money when Grant was completely broke. But Buckner had no choice—he surrendered to Grant.

The Union victories at Forts Henry and Donelson were the biggest things to happen in the war so far. With control of important rivers, Northern forces began driving deeper into Southern territory.

The victories also gave U.S. Grant a new nickname—"Unconditional Surrender" Grant. He had a new reputation as a man with a fierce determination to succeed. One Union officer said that Grant wore "an expression as if he had determined to drive his head through a brick wall, and was about to do it."

At the beginning of April 1862, Grant and his army were camped beside the Tennessee River, near a small church called Shiloh. He had about 40,000 soldiers, and another 35,000 were on their way to join him. Grant's plan was to launch a big attack as soon as those men arrived.

As usual, he wasn't thinking about what his enemy was up to.

Time to See the Elephant

His enemy was pretty busy. After losing those important river forts, Jefferson Davis was pressuring his Southern generals to go on the attack. "We have recently met with serious disasters," he said. "What the people want is a battle and a victory." General Albert Sidney Johnston got the job of attacking Grant.

Before sunrise on April 3, Johnston's soldiers woke to the sound of beating drums. Men scribbled quick notes to their families, like this one Joseph Lyman wrote to his wife: "Good-bye. If I do not write it will be because I am working or fighting or wounded or sick or dead."

The soldiers were given three days' worth of food—most of them ate it all right away. Then they set out on a rainy, muddy march to battle.

This was still early in the war, and most soldiers on both sides had never been in combat. (Many of them had not even learned how to use their rifles yet.) With a mixture of terror and excitement, they called combat "seeing the elephant." What would it be like to see the elephant? "I may run," one Southern soldier wrote. "But if I do I wish that some of our own men would shoot me down."

A young Union soldier named Edward Edes had similar worries, as he told his father, "I have a mortal dread of the battlefield, for I have never yet been nearer to one than to hear the cannon roar & have never seen a person die. I am afraid that the groans of the wounded & dying will make me shake."

Ready or not, 100,000 young men were about to see the elephant at Shiloh. "I have ordered a battle for daylight tomorrow," General Johnston told his officers on April 5. "And I intend to hammer 'em!"

The Shiloh Surprise

The next morning, while Grant's soldiers were yawning and cooking breakfast, Johnston's army charged out of the woods. Taken completely by surprise, Union soldiers ran around camp, shouting:

"The rebels are coming!"

"The rebs are out there thicker than fleas on a dog's back!"

"We are whipped! Cut to pieces!"

"Retreat! Save yourselves!"

Thousands of Union soldiers panicked, sprinting to the edge of the Tennessee River. Terrified men lay flat on the muddy riverbank, absolutely refusing to move. Some even leaped onto logs and started paddling across the water. Grant, who had sprained his ankle two days before, was racing around with a crutch tied to his horse. He kept passing more and more men running away from the battle and toward the river.

Unfortunately for the Confederates, winning can be just as confusing as losing for an untrained army. During the wild charge into the Union camp, Confederate regiments got mixed up and separated from their commanders. And when hungry Southern soldiers saw abandoned breakfasts cooking over campfires, many couldn't resist—they stopped to grab hunks of meat and slurp cups of coffee. One soldier was seen running around with a huge wheel of cheese stuck on his bayonet.

Another man grabbed a Union mule and jumped on its back. The mule suddenly took off at top speed, racing across the field toward a line of Union soldiers. Confederate men cheered this fearless charge: "Just look at that brave man, charging right in the jaws of death!"

But the guy on the mule was actually trying to stop the animal. "It arn't me, boys, it's this blarsted old mule," he yelled. "Whoa! Whoa!"

Into the Hornets' Nest

As the morning wore on, the two sides settled into some serious fighting. And the battle of Shiloh quickly turned into the biggest, bloodiest battle of the war so far. "Everywhere it was one never-ending, terrible roar," said a Union soldier. A Confederate soldier said, "Men fell around us like leaves." The air in one part of the battlefield was so thick with buzzing bullets that soldiers called it the "Hornets' Nest."

"I will lead you!" shouted the Confederate general Johnston as he charged his horse into the Hornet's Nest. The charge drove the Union soldiers back—but Johnston suddenly felt faint and nearly fell from his horse.

"General, are you hurt?" asked an officer.

"Yes, and I fear seriously," Johnston replied.

In the fury of combat, Johnston had not even felt the bullet that sliced open an artery behind his right knee. Now his boot was filled with blood, and more was flowing freely down his leg. Johnston got down from his horse and bled to death before help could arrive.

Darkness finally ended the fighting. The Confederates had backed Grant's army up against the Tennessee River. But the battle was far from over.

Lick 'Em Tomorrow

The Union general William Tecumseh Sherman had fought nonstop since morning. That night Sherman found General Grant sitting under a tree, smoking a cigar. The two friends had a quick strategy meeting, which began like this:

"Well, Grant, we've had the devil's own day of it, haven't we."

William Sherman

"Yes, yes [puffing on cigar]. Lick 'em tomorrow, though."

Ulysses S. Grant

That was Grant—always thinking about going on the attack. And he knew he would have the advantage the next day. As he spoke with Sherman, thousands of fresh Union soldiers were arriving in camp.

First everyone had to live through a night of pure horror. Heavy rain began falling and flashes of lightning lit up awful scenes on the battlefield. Everywhere lay dead bodies, and parts of bodies. Wounded men lay helpless in the pounding rain, calling out for help. And bombs exploded all night long as Union gunboats blasted an endless series of shells into the Confederate camp.

Grant launched a massive attack early the next morning—and his prediction proved correct. The exhausted Confederate soldiers were driven back, forced to retreat south to Mississippi. Shiloh was a victory for the North, though both sides ended up more or less where they started.

It was also a victory that left everyone in shock. In just two days, more than 23,000 men had been killed or wounded. More Americans were killed or wounded in two days at Shiloh than in the American Revolution, the War of 1812, and the Mexican War combined.

The terrible message of the battle of Shiloh was clear. The North and South had gotten themselves into a much bigger, much bloodier war than anyone had expected.

Two Miserable Presidents

There was always something to ruin Abraham Lincoln's day. Any time he got some good news, bad news was close behind. Grant's victory at Shiloh was a good thing, right? But then Northern newspapers and politicians started flooding Lincoln with complaints. They were furious that Grant's army had been taken by surprise at Shiloh. Some even charged that Grant had been drunk on the battlefield. Lincoln was suddenly under heavy pressure to fire his most successful general.

Miserable in Washington, D.C.

Abraham Lincoln listened patiently to the complaints about General Grant. Grant had made mistakes, Lincoln admitted. And he certainly had a drinking problem—though rumors of him drinking during battle were false. In any case, the Union desperately needed generals who were not afraid to attack. As Lincoln said of Grant, "I can't spare this man—he fights!"

The early months of 1862 brought more good news/bad news to Lincoln's desk. The good news: Union ships in the Gulf of Mexico entered the Mississippi River and began blasting their way north through Louisiana. In April, Union ships captured New Orleans, the South's busiest port and biggest city.

The bad news? As you might expect, the South's biggest city was full of Southerners. Union soldiers had a serious problem controlling this angry population—especially the women. "Oh! How I hate the Yankees!" cried one Southern woman. The women of New Orleans insulted Union soldiers and spat on them in the street. A few women even leaned out upstairs windows and emptied chamber pots onto soldiers' heads.

Then there was some good news: after eight months of delays, General George McClellan was finally ready to march his massive army toward Richmond. At least, he said he was ready. The bad news: McClellan's army was moving very slowly, very cautiously. Lincoln sent telegrams practically begging McClellan to get on with the attack. "He's got the slows," Lincoln groaned.

Miserable in Richmond

From Jefferson Davis's point of view, McClellan was moving fast enough. The Union army was approaching Richmond, and the entire city was beginning to panic. Davis decided that his wife, Varina, and their children should move to a safer location. But after they left, he lay awake nights, missing them terribly. "Oh, mother, Uncle Jeff is miserable," wrote Davis's niece when she came for a visit.

He had good reason to be. The losses at Shiloh and New Orleans were painful blows. And like Lincoln, Davis faced a constant stream of criticism from newspapers and political leaders. Unlike Lincoln, Davis took every insult personally. "I wish I could learn just to let people alone who snap at me," he wrote to Varina. Instead, he lashed back at anyone who dared to question him. "Jefferson Davis now treats all men as if they were idiotic insects," complained one Southern newspaper.

It hardly helped Davis's mood that the South was facing some major challenges in this war.

"The enemy greatly outnumber us, and have many advantages in moving their forces."

Jefferson Davis

The North simply had more of everything—more people, more soldiers, more railroads and ships, more factories to produce guns and ammunition. The South came up with some creative solutions, such as melting down church bells for metal to make cannons. Southern newspapers even urged families to save their urine—it contains a chemical needed to make gunpowder.

The South did have a few advantages, though. They were fighting on their own land, and soldiers always seem to fight extra hard when they're defending their homes. Also, when the war started, many of the country's most talented military leaders went south. Now that Union soldiers were closing in on Richmond, Jefferson Davis turned to two of those men: Robert E. Lee and Stonewall Jackson.

Jackson's Distraction

Robert E. Lee knew that 100,000 Union soldiers were marching toward Richmond. He looked over his maps and saw that there were another 40,000 Union soldiers in the nearby Shenandoah Valley. Somehow Lee had to keep them there—keep them from joining the attack on Richmond.

This was a job for the quiet and secretive Stonewall Jackson. Hiding his plans even from his own soldiers, Jackson began a series of quick, confusing marches back and forth across the Shenandoah Valley. His army of 17,000 kept showing up where Union generals least expected them. Jackson's men marched 350 miles in thirty days, winning battle after battle, capturing thousands of prisoners and badly needed guns.

The Union soldiers in the Shenandoah Valley were so worried about Stonewall, they never made it to Richmond. And Jackson became a Southern hero—though a slightly strange one. He was known to suck on lemons for hours at a time (especially during battle), and he refused to eat pepper, saying it made his left leg hurt. He also fell asleep at odd times. "He could sleep in any position," one of Jackson's staff members remembered, "in a chair, under fire, or on horseback."

Sure enough, as Jackson's exhausted army headed back to Richmond, Jackson fell fast asleep on his horse, rocking and swaying in the saddle. A young soldier, thinking this was some drunk guy, came up and shouted, "Hello! I say, old fellow, where did you get your liquor?"

Jackson woke suddenly and looked at the officers around him. "Mr. McGuire, did you speak to me? Captain Pendleton, did you? Somebody did."

The young soldier realized his mistake. "Good God! It's old Jack!" he shouted. He ran from the road, jumped over a fence, and sprinted across a field.

Jackson laughed. Then he got off his horse, lay down on the ground, and took a nap.

"La Belle Rebelle"

One of Jackson's secret weapons in the Shenandoah Valley was an eighteen-year-old spy named Belle Boyd.

Boyd had been living with her family in the valley when Union forces arrived in 1861. A bunch of Union soldiers celebrated the fourth of July by getting drunk and breaking into homes. They started shattering plates, blasting their guns through windows, and tossing furniture into the street. After smashing up Belle's home, they took out an American flag and prepared to fly it over the house.

"Men," warned Belle's mother, "every member of this household will die before that flag is raised over us."

One of the soldiers shoved Mrs. Boyd and spit out a string of violent curses. For Belle, that was it. "I could stand it no longer. . . ."

she wrote, "My blood was literally boiling in my veins. I drew out my pistol and shot him."

The soldier died, but Boyd escaped punishment—a Union court ruled she had acted in self-defense.

The next year, when Stonewall Jackson came to the valley, Boyd began gathering information and passing coded messages to Jackson's army. One day she found out that Union officers would be meeting in a nearby hotel. She hid in a closet on the floor above the meeting room and listened to everything through a crack in the floor.

Jackson's army was fighting its way into town, and Boyd now had valuable information about Union plans. She ran into the street to find someone to deliver the news to Jackson.

"No, no," said all the men she met. "You go."

There was no time to think about it—she took off running toward the sounds of battle. Union soldiers shot at her as she raced across the battlefield. A few bullets actually sliced through her dress without hitting her.

Belle Boyd

"The rifle-balls flew thick and fast about me, and more than one struck the ground so near my feet as to throw the dust in my eyes."

Southern soldiers cheered when she reached them. One officer recognized her and said, "Good God, Belle, you're here! What is it?"

Panting from her run, Boyd delivered the information. Then she ran back home.

After winning another key victory, Stonewall Jackson dashed off a quick note: "MISS BELLE BOYD: I thank you, for myself and for the army, for the immense service that you have rendered your country today. —Hastily, I am your Friend, T. J. JACKSON"

Belle Boyd continued spying (despite being thrown in prison a couple of times) and soon became famous all over the world. A French newspaper nicknamed her "La Belle Rebelle"—the beautiful rebel.

Whenever You're Ready, George

Now it's time to check in on General George McClellan. We haven't missed much—he's still inching forward. And Lincoln is still begging him to speed up. "You must act," Lincoln telegraphed.

"The time is very near when I shall attack Richmond," McClellan insisted.

But Mac wanted more information before moving forward. He turned to an inventor named Thaddeus Lowe, who had built huge balloons in which he could float hundreds of feet above the enemy camp. Since there was no way to control the balloons in the air, they were tied to the ground with very long ropes.

Early one morning the Union general Fitz John Porter decided to have a look at the Confederate camp. He climbed into the basket, inflated the balloon, and started floating up. Then there was a sudden CRACK!—the rope holding the balloon to the ground snapped in half. Thousands of sleepy Union soldiers looked up and saw General Porter leaning out of the basket, waving his hands and yelling something that no one could hear.

"Open the valve!" shouted Thaddeus Lowe, pointing up to a rope connected to the valve that would let out the hydrogen gas that made the balloon rise. Soldiers ran along under the balloon yelling, "The valve! The valve! Open the valve!" But Porter couldn't reach the valve. He kept floating up, up, and away . . . out over Confederate territory.

Deciding to make the best of it, Porter took out his telescope and started studying the enemy camp. Confederate soldiers shot at the balloon but couldn't reach it. Both armies watched in amazement as shifting winds blew Porter back and forth, finally sending him crashing into an army tent—luckily for him, a Union army tent. Porter climbed out from the folds of the deflated balloon, unhurt.

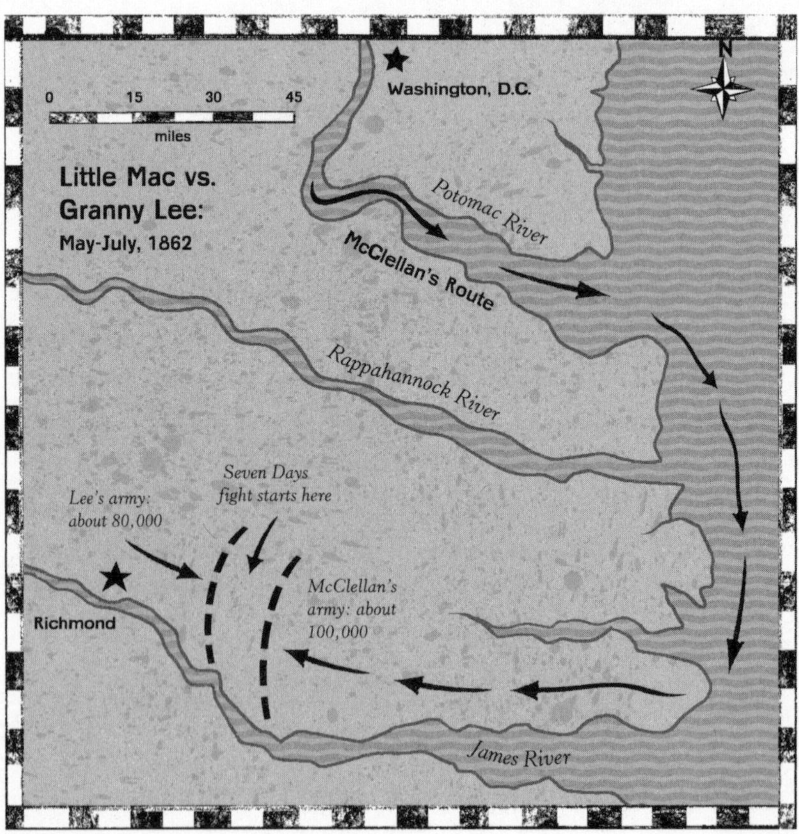

Seven Days with Granny Lee

Through the rainy, muddy May of 1862, McClellan's army continued pushing forward. By late May, Union forces were just six miles from Richmond. They could see the city's church steeples and hear the clocks striking. The men cheered when Mac visited them:

McClellan: *How do you feel, boys?*
Soldiers: *We feel bully, General!*
McClellan: *Do you think anything can stop you from going to Richmond?*
Soldiers: *No! No!*

Robert E. Lee disagreed.

With his polite manners, his white hair, and his glasses, Robert E. Lee didn't seem like a warrior. In fact, some folks in Richmond had taken to calling him "Granny Lee" (behind his back, of course). But soldiers who knew Lee painted a very different picture. As one Confederate officer said: "He will take more chances, and take them quicker, than any other general in this country, North or South."

Step one for Lee was to find out exactly where the enemy army was. He didn't have balloons, but he did have Jeb Stuart, a twenty-nine-year-old cavalry officer with a giant cinnamon-colored beard and a foot-long ostrich feather in his hat. Eager for action and fame, Stuart gladly accepted the dangerous mission of riding out and locating McClellan's army.

"And if I find the way open, it may be that I can ride all the way around him. Circle his whole army."

Jeb Stuart

And that's exactly what he did. Stuart led 1,200 men on a three-day, hundred-mile ride around McClellan's entire army. Losing just one man, Stuart's force burned wagons full of Union supplies and brought back hundreds of Union prisoners. Stuart got famous. McClellan got embarrassed. And Lee got the information he needed.

Then, in a series of brutal battles known as the Seven Days, Lee attacked McClellan every day for a week. "Come on, come on, my men! Do you want to live forever?" shouted a Confederate officer to his charging soldiers. The Union soldiers staggered backwards, fighting their guts out but steadily losing ground. The casualties were enormous—a total of more than 30,000 Union and Confederate soldiers were killed or wounded. And though Lee lost even more men than McClellan, Seven Days was a major Confederate victory. The Union army had been driven far from Richmond.

When the fighting ended, survivors on both sides tried to put the weeklong bloodbath behind them. One Southern soldier remembered: "Our boys and the Yanks made a bargain not to fire at each other, and went out in the field . . . and gathered berries together and talked over the fight, traded tobacco and coffee and exchanged newspapers as peacefully and kindly as if they had not been engaged for the last seven days in butchering each other."

What About Slavery?

Abraham Lincoln was in no mood to pick berries. The entire North was disappointed and angry, and Lincoln got most of the blame. He desperately wanted to fire McClellan, but he was afraid the soldiers would be angry. "McClellan has the army with him," Lincoln said.

Then there was the always explosive issue of slavery. Abolitionists such as Frederick Douglass were demanding that Lincoln attack Southern slavery as well as Southern armies.

"To fight against slaveholders, without fighting against slavery, is but a half-hearted business."

Frederick Douglass

Douglass was making an interesting point about war strategy. Southern farms and businesses depended on the labor of enslaved African Americans. And the Southern army was using slaves to build forts and cook food. Slavery was actually helping the South fight the war. So freeing slaves could help the North win it.

Lincoln agreed with Douglass's logic. When asked about ending slavery, he said, "I can assure you that the subject is on my mind, by day and night, more than any other."

One of the questions on Lincoln's worried mind was this: If the Confederacy's 3.5 million slaves were freed, where would they live? Lincoln was considering an idea some politicians were suggesting—that freed slaves should move to another country, maybe in Central America. But black leaders came to the White House to urge Lincoln to put that stupid idea out of his mind. As Robert Purvis told the president: "In the matter of rights, there is but one race, and that is the human race. . . . Sir, this is our country as much as it is yours, and we will not leave it."

Lincoln was also nervous about the four "border states," or slave states that were still in the Union: Missouri, Kentucky, Maryland, and Delaware. If he tried to abolish slavery, would those states join the Confederacy?

And here's another question: Shouldn't free African Americans be allowed to enlist in the Union army? As of the middle of 1862, this was still being debated in Congress.

Some people weren't waiting for Congress to make up its mind.

Robert Smalls's Dash to Freedom

Robert Smalls was a twenty-three-year-old expert boat pilot in Charleston, South Carolina. He was also a slave. In 1862, Smalls was working on the *Planter,* an armed steamship used by the Confederate navy.

On the night of May 12, the *Planter* was loaded with weapons and ammunition. The captain told Smalls to have the ship ready for an early departure the next morning.

"Aye, aye, sir," Smalls said.

The captain and white crew went on shore for the night, leaving on board Smalls and the other black crew members. The captain never would have guessed that Smalls and the black crew, all slaves, had spent the past few months preparing for this exact moment.

At three a.m. on May 13, Smalls put on the captain's hat and jacket. He powered up the steam engines and began cruising—very slowly, as if this were just another normal night. At a dark waterside spot he stopped to pick up his wife and children, as well as family members of the other crew members. Then he turned the ship and headed out to sea.

Now came the most dangerous part of the escape: the *Planter* had to sail right past five Confederate forts in the harbor. To pass each fort, a ship had to blow a different secret signal on its steam whistle. Smalls knew these signals, but if anything went wrong, he and the crew had agreed, they would never allow themselves to be taken alive. If stopped, they would blow the ship into the sky.

Smalls hunched over and paced back and forth exactly as the *Planter*'s captain normally did. Smalls had practiced this walk, and in the dark, from a distance, he looked like the captain. As the ship passed each fort, Smalls blew all the right signals on the ship's whistle. At 4:15, just as the sun was beginning to rise, the *Planter* reached Fort Sumter, the last fort. Smalls blew the secret signal.

"Pass!" yelled the guard.

Safely beyond the fort, Smalls ran a white flag (the signal of truce or surrender) up the ship's flagpole and sailed toward a group of Union ships floating about three miles out. As the *Planter* cruised closer, Union sailors were shocked to see a Confederate ship with an all-black crew. A Union captain demanded to speak with the *Planter*'s captain.

You're speaking with him now, Robert Smalls told them. "I have the honor, sir, to present the *Planter*."

Robert Smalls's dash to freedom was a massive front-page story all over the North and South. It was "one of the most daring and heroic adventures" of the war, declared the *New York Herald*. The Union gained a valuable ship, full of supplies. And Smalls became a symbol in the debate over emancipation. To many Northerners, Smalls's actions made it more obvious than ever that all African Americans should be free.

Lincoln Is Convinced

In a meeting with his cabinet on July 22, 1862, Lincoln announced an important decision. He was going to declare all slaves in the Confederacy free.

Once they got over the shock, most of Lincoln's advisors supported the idea. But the secretary of state, William Seward, raised a concern. If they issued this plan now, when the war was going so badly for them, wouldn't they look kind of weak and desperate? Wouldn't it be better to wait for a military victory?

Good point, Lincoln said. He put the Emancipation Proclamation back in his desk.

In August there was another big battle near Bull Run in Virginia. Lee and Jackson crushed a large Northern force, sending the Union army stumbling back toward Washington.

"Well, John, we are whipped again, I'm afraid," Lincoln told his secretary. And that proclamation stayed in his desk.

Lee's Hungry Wolves

Remember that quote about Robert E. Lee taking chances? On September 4, Lee's army waded into the Potomac River and splashed across the shallow water to Maryland. Lee was invading the North.

Lee knew he could lose everything—his entire army, and the war too. But he also knew he could win everything. One huge victory on Northern territory just might convince the North that it could never win this war. The South would have its independence.

There was only one problem, as Lee told Jefferson Davis, "The army is not properly equipped for an invasion of an enemy's territory."

That was putting it mildly. Thousands of Lee's soldiers were barefoot. Their clothes and bodies were so filthy, people in Maryland said they smelled the army before they saw it. One witness called them "the dirtiest men I ever saw, a most ragged, lean, and hungry set of wolves." Lee's half-starved soldiers picked unripe apples and corn, and soon thousands of men were sprinting into the woods, sick with diarrhea.

Still, Lee's soldiers continued marching north in high spirits. These were tough combat veterans who were used to winning.

Then, in a war full of incredible events, something truly unbelievable happened.

Who Dropped the Cigars?

A few days after Lee's army marched through Frederick, Maryland, the Union army began to arrive. At about ten in the morning on September 13, a group of Indiana soldiers sat down to grab a quick rest. Corporal Barton Mitchell was sitting under a tree when he noticed a piece of paper lying in the grass a few feet away. He picked up the paper and found that it was wrapped around three cigars. Barton was thrilled—he sent his friend for matches to light the cigars. Then he unrolled the piece of paper. "As I read, each line became more interesting," he said. "I forgot those cigars."

Special Orders, No. 191

Headquarters Army of Northern Virginia

. . . The army will resume its march tomorrow, taking the Hagerstown road. General Jackson's command will form the advance . . .

This was General Lee's entire plan! Some careless Southern officer must have wrapped a copy of the plan around his cigars and dropped it there by accident. The letter described exactly where each part of Lee's army was and where they were headed. And best of all, it showed that Lee's army was spread out all over the place—completely unprepared for battle.

"Now I know what to do!" shouted McClellan when he saw the letter. "Here is a paper with which, if I cannot whip Bobby Lee, I will be willing to go home."

Southern spies told Lee that McClellan had his plans. Lee rushed messages to all his commanders to gather as quickly as possible at a town called Sharpsburg. When Lee got there he pointed to the high ground above Antietam Creek and said, "We will make our stand on these hills."

McClellan, meanwhile, moved so slowly that he missed a golden opportunity to attack before Lee was ready. By September 17, Lee had about 40,000 soldiers at Antietam Creek. Little Mac had about 80,000.

Families hid in their cellars and frightened farmers cleared their cows and horses from the fields.

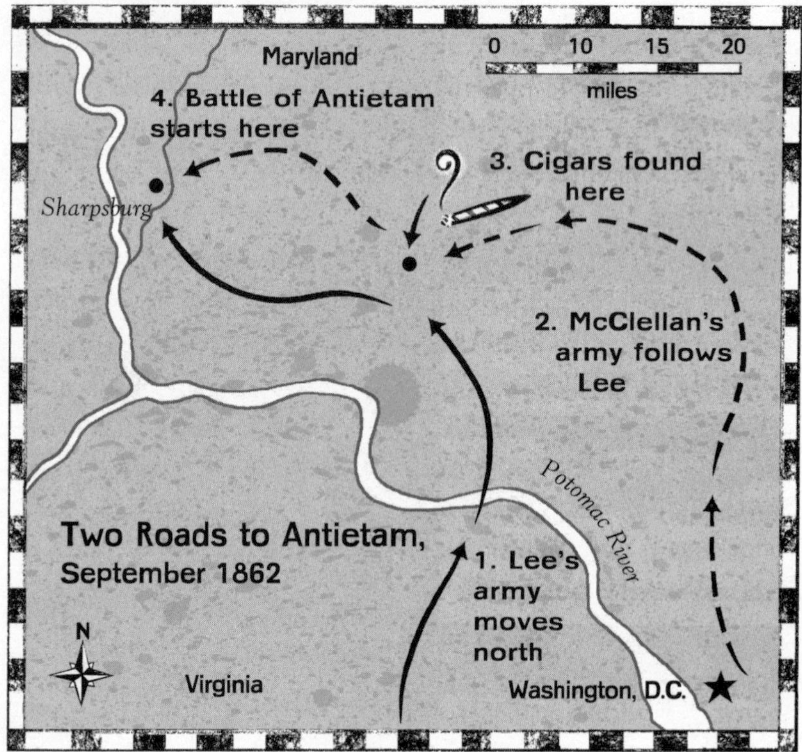

Into the Awful Tornado

When the armies woke before sunrise on September 17, a milky mist covered the fields near Antietam Creek. Sleepy soldiers began the day by wiping the dew from their rifles.

A group of Texas soldiers had just begun cooking breakfast (their first hot meal in three days) when they were ordered into battle. "I have never seen a more disgusted bunch of boys and mad as hornets," one soldier said.

Union soldiers were building fires and boiling coffee when the first Southern shell came screaming into camp. A soldier named Albert Monroe said: "Every one dropped whatever he had in his hands, and looked around the group to see whose head was missing."

No one's was—yet. But another huge and horrible battle was under way.

All day the armies charged at each other, driving one another back and forth across a large cornfield and a dirt road that became known as the "Bloody Lane." Entire rows of men were cut down as they charged at enemy guns, and arms and legs were blasted thirty feet into the air. "A man but a few paces from me is struck squarely in the face by a solid shot," recalled George Kimball of Massachusetts. "Fragments of the poor fellow's head come crashing into my face and fill me with disgust." Kimball wiped his face and continued fighting.

After a few hours, soldiers said they could have walked across the battlefield on fallen bodies without ever touching the ground. "A savage continual thunder that cannot compare to any sound I ever heard" was how Charles Johnson of New York described the fight at Antietam.

"The earth and sky seemed to be on fire," said a Texan named W.R. Hamby.

"It seemed as if a million bees were singing in the air," said Charles Tanner of Delaware.

Another soldier spoke of "the awful tornado of battle."

In the middle of the storm was a Union army nurse named Clara Barton. Hunched over to avoid the flying metal, Barton raced from one wounded soldier to the next. When she lifted one wounded man's head to give him a drink of water, a bullet ripped through her sleeve and hit the soldier, killing him. "I have never mended that hole in my sleeve," she later said.

She found another man lying on the ground with a bullet stuck in his cheekbone. "It is terribly painful," he told her. "Won't you take it out?"

There was no time to wait for a surgeon. Barton took out her pocketknife. Another wounded man, shot in both legs, offered to help with the operation.

"And shoving himself along upon the ground he took the wounded head in his hands and held it while I extracted the ball and washed and bandaged the face."*

Clara Barton

Then she moved on. And on, and on. "Oh! God—what a costly war," she wrote in her journal.

Mac vs. Lincoln

More than 25,000 men were killed or wounded in the battle of Antietam, making it the bloodiest single day of the entire Civil War. In fact, more Americans died that day than on any other day in American history, before or since. Both sides suffered a similar number of casualties. But since Lee's army was smaller, it was in much worse shape after the battle. Lee had no choice but to turn around and head south.

* *removed*

"The enemy is driven back into Virginia," bragged McClellan. "Those on whose judgment I rely tell me that I fought the battle splendidly and that it was a masterpiece of the art."

But from Abraham Lincoln's point of view, McClellan's much larger army should have crushed Lee. And after the battle, Mac should have leaped at the chance to destroy Lee's crippled army as it retreated across the Potomac. Instead, he let Lee slip safely back into Virginia.

Over the next few weeks, an increasingly furious Lincoln kept ordering McClellan to cross the Potomac and attack Lee. But McClellan complained his horses were "too fatigued" (tired, that is). Abe snapped back, "Will you pardon me for asking what the horses of your army have done since the Battle of Antietam that fatigues anything?"

Mac grumbled to his wife, "There never was a truer epithet applied to a certain individual than that of the 'Gorilla.'"

Lincoln was finally fed up—he removed McClellan from command. Little Mac went home to New Jersey. But don't worry. He'll be back in the story later.

The Time Has Come

Antietam was not the rebellion-smashing victory Lincoln had been dreaming of—but it was still a victory. It was good enough. Now Lincoln felt he could announce his emancipation plan. "I think the time has come," he said.

On September 22, 1862, Lincoln announced the Emancipation Proclamation. Here's the key passage:

"On the first day of January, in the year of our Lord One Thousand Eight Hundred and Sixty-Three, all persons held as slaves within any State or designated part of a State, the people whereof shall then be in rebellion against the United States, shall be then, thenceforward, and forever free."

Okay, this is not the most clearly worded statement ever written. But you get the idea—as of January 1, 1863, all slaves in the Confederacy would be free.

Except for one problem: Lincoln had no power in the states that had seceded from the Union. So slave owners in the Confederacy could simply ignore Lincoln's announcement. And the Emancipation Proclamation did not free slaves in states still in the Union. (Lincoln felt this would require an amendment to the Constitution.)

So when it was issued, the Emancipation Proclamation did not actually emancipate anyone. And yet it changed everything. Up until this point in the Civil War, the North had been fighting to save the Union. From now on, the North would be fighting to save the Union and to end slavery.

That didn't mean the North was going to win.

Johnny Reb vs. Billy Yank

Bob McIntosh needed a haircut. This young Southern soldier had wild curly hair that shot out in all directions. So one quiet day in Virginia, Bob sat down on a tree stump and a soldier named Van started snipping with his scissors. Van shaved the right side of Bob's head down to the scalp, leaving the left side covered with long black curls. Van was about to begin cutting the left side when a soldier ran up shouting: "Get your guns! The Yankees are across the river!"

Bob's Half Haircut

Bob McIntosh's haircut was over. He jumped up from the log and raced toward his cannon, a towel still tied around his neck and his half head of curly hair flapping in the breeze. Suddenly he realized how ridiculous he must look. He turned to his friend William Dame and said, "Good heavens, Billy, it has just come to me what a devil of a fix I am in with my head in this condition. I tell you now that if the Yankees get too close to the guns I am going to run. . . . I wouldn't be caught dead with my head looking like this."

Enemy bombs started flying toward them and exploding all around. Bob and his friends went to work on their cannons, loading, firing, cleaning, and reloading as fast as they could. The only problem was, they all kept looking over at Bob—and they couldn't stop laughing. "I caught sight of that half-shaved head," William Dame said, "and it was the funniest object you ever saw."

When the short battle ended, Van couldn't find his scissors. At least, he said he couldn't. Bob tried to cut his own hair with a knife, but the blade was too dull. After a week of looking like a clown, he got so desperate, he asked a soldier named Hunter to cut his hair with an ax.

"All right, Bob," Hunter said, "put your head on this stump and I'll chop off some of your hair."

Bob put his head on the stump and Hunter swung down with his ax—but the blade got stuck in the wood, painfully pinning Bob's hair to the stump.

"He began to call Hunter all the names he could think of," William Dame said.

"Why, Bob," Hunter said, "you couldn't expect me to cut your hair with a hatchet without hurting some."

Van finally "found" his scissors and finished the haircut.

Soldier life was not usually this entertaining. In fact, Civil War soldiers said they were usually pretty bored. They passed the time in camp by writing letters and reading, by playing cards and singing and putting on shows. They played baseball, held wrestling tournaments, and bowled with cannonballs.

Of course, they also spent a lot of time just talking. A Texas man spoke for soldiers North and South when he named the two most popular topics of conversation. Can you guess what they were?

Hungry All the Time

One was "wives and sweethearts." The other was "something to eat."

When you read letters and diaries of Civil War soldiers, you realize that these men were hungry almost all the time. Carlton McCarthy talked about food shortages in the Southern army: "To be one day without anything to eat was common. Two days' fasting, marching, and fighting was not uncommon, and there were times when no rations were issued for three or four days."

When the men did get enough food, it was often unhealthy, or plain old rotten. "The beef is so poor, it is sticky and blue," a Southern soldier wrote. Both armies relied heavily on salted beef and pork—the salt was supposed to keep the meat from rotting. But it also turned the meat into tough, salty slabs. Union soldiers called the stuff "salt horse."

A young soldier from Illinois described another common problem: "Very few of us knew anything whatever about cooking." When he and his friends got a little flour, they tried making pancakes. But they turned out "tough as a mule's ear, about as heavy as lead."

Hungry soldiers often spent their own money on a little extra food. A Texas soldier named William Fletcher remembered buying a sausage and biting into something surprisingly crunchy. "I found what I supposed was a cat's claw," he said. He stopped eating the sausage. "An examination was hurriedly made of the uneaten portion, and a cat's tooth was discovered." Soldiers who had no extra money sometimes became desperate. "Once I took some corn from my horse, beat it between stones and tried to swallow it," a Southern soldier said.

The Union soldiers' diet was based mainly on hardtack—dried wheat biscuits, or "sheet iron crackers," as soldiers called them. They were so hard, soldiers had to smash them up with the butts of their rifles before attempting to eat them. Then they mixed the crumbled hardtack into their soup, or fried it up with the grease from their meat. "We had fifteen different ways of preparing them," a Minnesota teenager proudly recalled.

John Billings of Massachusetts remembered that the most popular way to eat hardtack was to crumble it up into coffee. One problem: hardtack was often home to weevils and maggots and other bugs. "It was no uncommon occurrence for a man to find the surface of his pot of coffee swimming with weevils . . ." he said, "but they were easily skimmed off and left no distinctive flavor behind."

That gives you an idea of how hungry these boys were.

Almost Time for War

Now it's time to get back to the fighting . . . almost. You'll recall that Abraham Lincoln removed General George McClellan from command of the Army of the Potomac. In November 1862, Lincoln gave the command to General Ambrose Burnside.

Burnside protested that he was not the right man for this job. People sometimes say things like this just to sound humble. In this case, Burnside was telling the truth. Never known for his brilliance on the battlefield, Burnside was much more famous for his facial hair. In fact, he even inspired a new word for facial hair: sideburns.

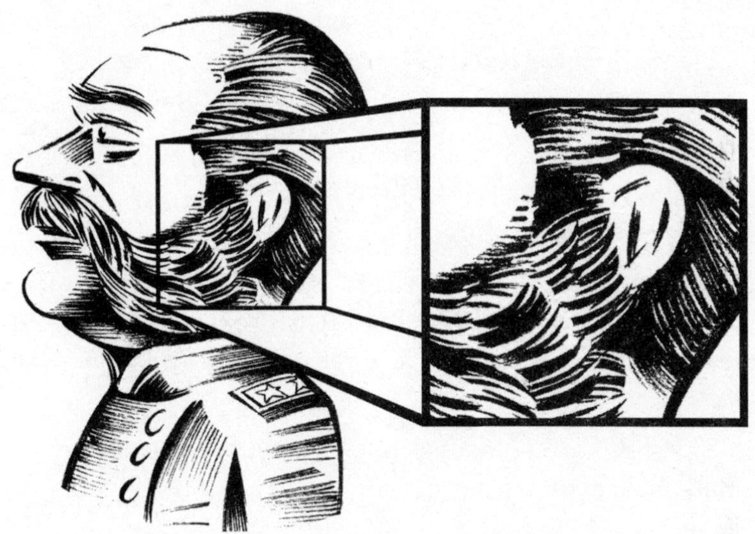

Burnside had always been a bit unlucky. On his wedding day years before, the minister asked Burnside's fiancée, Lottie Moon, if she would take him to be her lawfully wedded husband.

"No-siree-bob!" Lottie sang, and walked out of the church.

Now Burnside had more than 100,000 Union soldiers lined up near the town of Fredericksburg, Virginia, on the north bank of the Rappahannock River. He wanted to cross the river and attack Robert E. Lee's army. But the portable bridges he needed had not yet arrived, and no one knew when they would get there. So Burnside just waited. And this gave Lee plenty of time to get his army ready.

Meanwhile, Northern and Southern soldiers were only separated by a river. One morning Alexander Hunter of Virginia heard voices from across the river—someone was yelling "Johnny Reb! Johnny Reb!" (Northerners called Southern soldiers "Johnny Reb." Southerners called Northern soldiers "Billy Yank.")

Billy Yank: *Johnny Reb! I say, Johnny Reb, don't shoot!*
Johnny Reb: *All right! Come out on the bank and show yourselves; we won't fire.*
Billy Yank: *On your honor, Johnny Reb?*
Johnny Reb: *On our honor, Billy Yank.*

Soldiers from both sides walked down to the river's edge and looked at each other across the water. Then they began talking trades.

Billy Yank: *Have you any tobacco?*
Johnny Reb: *Plenty of it.*
Billy Yank: *Say, Johnny, want some newspapers?*
Johnny Reb: *Yes!*
Billy Yank: *Then look out, we are going to send you some.*
Johnny Reb: *How are you going to do it?*
Billy Yank: *Wait and see.*

The Northern soldiers had built several tiny sailboats, each one just big enough to hold a couple newspapers. They set the boats on the water and the wind blew them across the river.

Soon the whole river was dotted with tiny trading ships bobbing back and forth. New Jersey soldiers picked up a six-inch boat from the water and found this note from Mississippi men:

"Gents, U.S. Army: We send you some tobacco by our packet. Send us some coffee in return. Also a deck of cards if you have them, and we will send you more tobacco."

Then the Union's portable bridges finally arrived. Burnside ordered his army to cross the Rappahannock and attack Lee's army.

Burnside Blows It

Robert E. Lee could hardly believe his eyes.

He had his entire army in perfect position—lined up behind stone walls on the tops of hills. And Burnside was about to march his men across a huge open field right up to Lee's rifles and cannons! "What luck some people have," grumbled a jealous Joseph Johnson, commander of Confederate forces in the West. "Nobody will ever come to attack me in such a place."

Burnside really should have come up with a better plan. But he didn't. And early on the foggy morning of December 13, 1862, Union men started marching across the open field.

From their hilltop positions Lee's men looked down at the field and saw only fog. But they could hear the Union army under that fog: snorting horses, rolling wagon wheels, pounding drums. Then the fog began to burn off and Confederate soldiers saw thousands of blue-coated Union soldiers marching toward them, their colorful flags flapping in the wind. Many Southerners said that it was a beautiful sight.

Then it turned ugly.

As they marched uphill toward the Southern guns, Union soldiers were shot down in entire rows. Still, more soldiers kept coming. John McCrillis remembered that his New Hampshire regiment was ordered into action at about noon. "If I fall, never mind me," Colonel Edward Cross told the men. "Forward, march!"

The men marched into what McCrillis described as a "rain of death" and "a stream of fire and a shower of leaded hail." Soldiers fell in bunches. Soon Colonel Cross was wounded and he lay helpless on the ground.

> *"My mouth was full of blood, fragments of teeth, and gravel; my breastbone almost broken in; and I lay in mud two inches deep."*
>
> **Edward Cross**

McCrillis saw Colonel Cross go down, along with almost everyone else in his regiment. There was no one left to give orders. "At this time there was no one in sight to my right or left, except the dead or wounded." McCrillis was hit in the arm and retreated to the rear.

This kind of thing continued all day. Fresh Union soldiers marched forward, faced the deadly Confederate fire, and were blown backwards. Wounded Union soldiers who were lying on the ground actually reached up to grab the legs of advancing soldiers, trying to stop more men from marching into a hopeless attack.

Oh, Those Men!

General Lee watched his army win an easy victory at the battle of Fredericksburg. It was so easy, he had to remind himself that combat was not supposed to be fun. He turned to General James Longstreet and said, "It is well that war is so terrible—or we should grow too fond of it."

There was no danger of Burnside becoming too fond of war. That night he paced back and forth in his tent, pointing to the blood-soaked battlefield and crying over and over, "Oh, those men! Those men over there! I am thinking of them all the time!"

There were a lot of them to think about. More than 12,000 Union soldiers were killed or wounded at Fredericksburg. Lee lost about 4,000 men.

Surgeons on both sides were busy for days. Men who were badly wounded in the vital organs of the chest or stomach had little chance of surviving. Doctors simply did not know how to deal with these kinds of wounds. So surgeons spent much of their time working on smashed arms and legs, often by cutting them off. The best army surgeons could amputate a limb in about ten minutes.

Soldiers got used to seeing amputated arms and legs piling up outside battlefield hospitals. But a Union soldier named William Hamilton saw something especially disgusting at Fredericksburg. "There was a hospital within thirty yards of us," Hamilton wrote to his mother. "About the building you could see the hogs belonging to the farm eating arms and other portions of the body."

Sadly, soldiers who had their arms or legs amputated did not always get healthy. Doctors in the 1860s understood a little about germs, but they didn't know how to kill the germs on their hands or instruments. "We operated in old blood-stained and often pus-stained coats," said one Union army surgeon. Surgeons stuck their ungloved fingers into wounds to feel for bullets. If they dropped a sponge or saw on the floor, they simply wiped it off with a cloth, or "washed" it in a basin of bloody water. As a result, about twenty-five percent of the soldiers who had an arm or leg amputated later died from infections.

Worse Than Bullets

Soldiers who were lucky enough to avoid getting shot still faced the most dangerous killer of all in the Civil War—disease. Deadly diseases such as typhoid fever and dysentery spread through the camps of both Northern and Southern soldiers. By the time the war was over, twice as many men had died from disease as from battle wounds.

A big part of the problem was the fact that army camps were often disgustingly dirty, allowing germs to spread quickly. For bathrooms, the men dug shallow, open ditches right near their tents. The ditches filled up quickly and got so gross that many of the men preferred to do their business elsewhere. A Virginia soldier found this out the hard way, as he wrote in his diary: "On rolling up my bed this morning I found that I had been lying in—I won't say what—something though that didn't smell like milk and peaches."

Rotting food, animal manure, and dead animals also piled up all over camp. And this stuff seeped through the ground into streams and wells, polluting the water the soldiers drank. At one army camp, a newspaper reporter wrote, the water "smells so offensively that the men have to hold their noses while drinking it." That can't be good for you.

The lack of personal cleanliness was another problem. Union army soldiers were supposed to wash their hands and face every day, their feet twice a week, and their whole body once a week. But not everyone did this. George H. Cadman from Ohio remembered that some of the men in his regiment were especially filthy, and "if not pretty sharply looked after would not wash themselves from week's end to week's end.

"There are two brothers who are especially dirty and if they are left alone for a few days they get such a coat of dirt upon their faces it is impossible to tell one from the other."

Civil War soldiers were always short on soap, and many went weeks without washing or changing their clothes. "Soap seems to have given out entirely in the Confederacy," said a Southern soldier. "I am without drawers [underwear] today, both pair of mine being so dirty that I can't stand them." The Union soldier John Billings knew some men who remembered to change their underwear "at least once a week." But others, he said, "would do so only under the severest pressure."

One result of wearing dirty clothes was that Civil War soldiers fought a never-ending battle against body lice. Every night in camp, men sat around the fire picking lice off their clothes. The only way to really get rid of lice was to take off all your clothes and boil them in one of the kettles used for cooking food. But that was a lot of trouble—and the lice came back soon anyway.

Now you can understand why Civil War soldiers were often eager to leave camp, even if it meant marching into battle.

Fighting Joe's Turn

After the disaster at Fredericksburg, Abraham Lincoln had no choice but to remove General Burnside from command. The war was going so badly that some people in the North were urging Lincoln to give up the fight. "We are now on the brink of destruction," he said.

It was about to get worse.

Still searching for someone who could lead the Army of the Potomac to victories, Lincoln decided to give General Joseph Hooker a chance. Known to his men as "Fighting Joe," Hooker boldly declared he would march right to Richmond.

"My plans are perfect, and when I start to carry them out, may God have mercy on General Lee, for I will have none."

"Fighting Joe" Hooker

Lincoln winced when he heard such stupid statements. "That is the most depressing thing about Hooker," he complained. "It seems to me that he is overconfident."

Hooker had good reason to be confident, though—he had about twice as many soldiers as Lee. In late April 1863 Hooker began marching his army through a thick Virginia forest known as the Wilderness. He camped near the town of Chancellorsville.

Lee Throws Out the Textbook

Once again, Robert E. Lee took a huge risk. According to the military textbooks Lee studied in college, when you have a smaller army than your enemy, you should keep all your soldiers together. Ignoring the rules, Lee divided his army into even smaller pieces. He gave a piece to Stonewall Jackson and told him to launch a surprise attack. "It must be victory or death," Lee said.

On the morning of May 2, Jackson led his men on a long march to get in position for the attack. "Press on, press forward!" he urged, as the army raced along narrow roads.

This was Hooker's big chance—he could have charged forward and crushed Lee's divided army. Instead, he just sat there. Later, when asked what had gone wrong, he said, "Well to tell the truth, I just lost confidence in Joe Hooker." Bad timing, Joe.

At 5:15 that afternoon, Union soldiers were relaxing around their campfires, cooking dinner and playing cards. Then something very strange happened—dozens of rabbits and deer suddenly burst out of the nearby woods and ran into the army camp. The men waved their hats and cheered the charging animals. That was the wrong reaction.

The reason those animals ran into the Union camp was that Stonewall Jackson's army was right behind them, driving them forward through the woods. Jackson's men charged into the Union camp, screaming the rebel yell. Startled Union soldiers were driven back into the woods.

What followed was part violent battle and part confusing chase through the forest. Whatever it was, Jackson was winning, and the fighting lasted until dark.

Another Union Disaster

The battle of Chancellorsville continued the next morning, getting closer and closer to the Chancellor family house, which General Hooker was using as his headquarters. Fourteen-year-old Sue Chancellor, along with her mother and five sisters, dashed to the cellar for safety. Then a Union officer ran down and told them to get out—the house was on fire!

Sue scrambled out into the daylight and was met with a shocking scene. "The woods around the house were a sheet of fire," she said. "Horses were running, rearing, and screaming, the men, a mass of confusion, moaning, cursing, and praying. Cannon were booming and missiles of death were flying in every direction. . . . If anybody thinks that a battle is an orderly attack of rows of men, I can tell them differently, for I have been there."

Sue and her family retreated to a safer spot. So did "Fighting Joe" Hooker and most of his army. The battle of Chancellorsville was another crushing defeat for the Union.

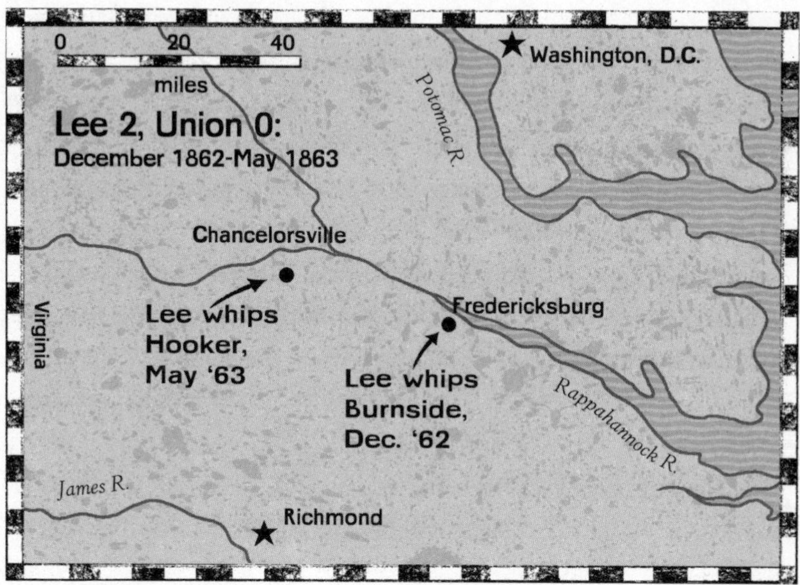

Jackson Crosses the River

"At Chancellorsville we gained another victory," Lee said. "Our people were wild with delight." But there was a dark side to the victory. "Our losses were severe," Lee explained.

Lee's army lost about 13,000 men, compared with 17,000 for the Union. But remember, the South had a much smaller population than the North. So Lee knew he would have a much harder time replacing soldiers. He simply could not afford such bloody victories.

And the news got worse. The night after his successful surprise attack, Stonewall Jackson was riding through the dark woods, planning the next day's action. A group of Confederate soldiers mistook him for a Union officer and fired, hitting Jackson in the right hand and left arm. Jackson was carried back to camp, where a surgeon amputated his shattered arm.

Jackson was recovering from the operation when he developed pneumonia. It became clear that he was dying. Lee reacted strangely, refusing to visit Jackson—refusing to face the fact that he was about to lose his best fighter. "He has lost his left arm, but I have lost my right," Lee said. "Tell him to make haste and get well, and come back to me as soon as he can."

Anna Jackson was more realistic. She rushed to her husband's hospital bed. "His fearful wounds, his mutilated arm, the scratches on his face, and, above all, the desperate pneumonia . . ." she said, "wrung my soul with such grief and anguish as it had never before experienced."

When Stonewall asked Anna how he was doing, Anna spoke the harsh truth. Stonewall called over Dr. Hunter McGuire.

"Doctor," he said. "Anna informs me that you have told her I am to die today. Is it so?"

Dr. McGuire nodded.

"It is all right. It is the Lord's day," Jackson said. "I always desired to die on Sunday."

Soon he began drifting into dreams, calling out battle orders to his generals: "Order A.P. Hill to prepare for action!" Then he smiled and quietly said, "Let us cross over the river, and rest under the shade of the trees." Then he died.

Jefferson Davis declared a national day of mourning throughout the South.

What Will the Country Say!

If you think Jefferson Davis was depressed, wait till you hear about Abraham Lincoln.

A journalist named Noah Brooks was with Lincoln when a telegram arrived describing Hooker's defeat at Chancellorsville. As Lincoln read the paper, Brooks watched the president's face turn a sickly gray.

"Never, as long as I knew him, did he seem to be so broken, so dispirited, so ghostlike," Brooks said.

Lincoln clasped his hands behind his back and started pacing back and forth, saying:

"My God! My God! What will the country say!

What will the country say!"

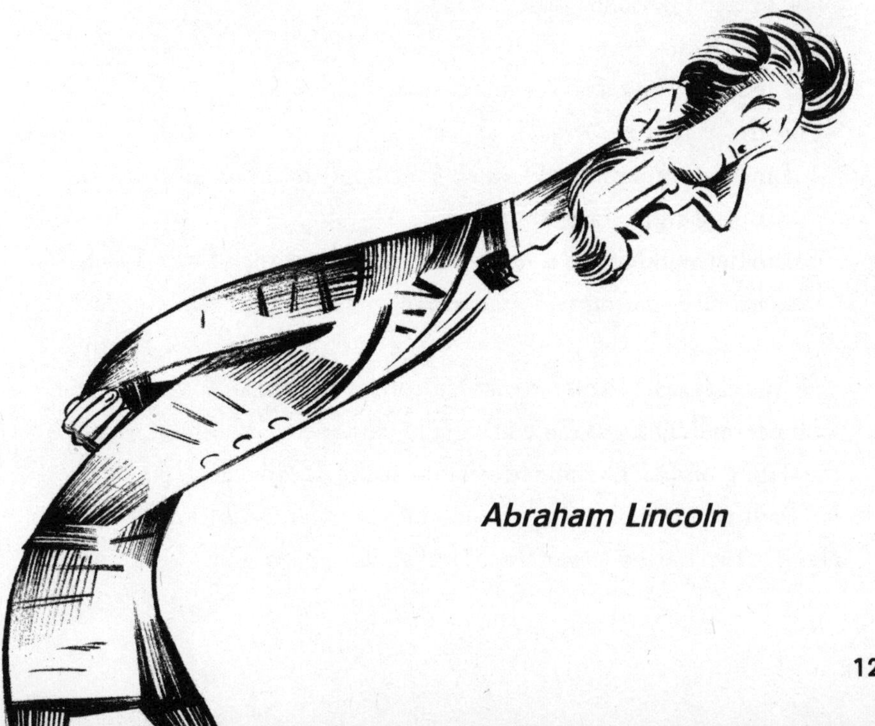

Abraham Lincoln

The country said a lot—some of it too rude to print here. The basic idea was that Lincoln was messing up, he was losing the war. More and more people were calling for Lincoln to admit defeat and let the South have its independence. But Lincoln was as determined as ever to preserve the Union.

While trying to figure out exactly how to do that, Lincoln had to deal with the annoying day-to-day details of his job. Unlike today, anyone could walk right into the White House and ask to meet the president. Even in the middle of the war, tourists, honeymooners, and soldiers lined up to meet Lincoln and shake his hand. People came to show him inventions or ask for jobs in the government. One guy showed up asking to be made ambassador to Germany or France. When he was told those positions were taken, the man said, "Well, then, will you lend me five dollars?"

A teenage boy complained that he had been hired to deliver horses to Washington. He did the job, but his boss never paid him. Now he had no money to get home.

Lincoln: *What do you want me to do?*
Kid: *I want you to send me home.*
Lincoln: *I have no fund which I can apply to such a purpose.*
Kid: *I don't know what to do.*
Lincoln: *I'll tell you what I would have done when I was a young fellow like you. I would have worked my own way back.*

Another man wanted to use Lincoln's name in an advertisement. The normally patient Lincoln finally exploded. "You have come to the wrong place," he shouted. "There is the door!"

In June 1863 Lincoln got something much more serious to worry about—Lee's army was in the North again.

The Road to Gettysburg

Following up his victories in Virginia, General Lee decided to try another invasion of the North. He knew that Northerners were getting discouraged and tired of war. And he hoped that one more Southern victory would convince them to give up the fight.

This was a very real possibility, and Lincoln knew it. He did not want the fate of the nation resting in the shaky hands of "Fighting Joe" Hooker. So he changed generals again!

On the night of June 28, a Union general named George Meade was fast asleep in his tent. At about three a.m. Meade heard someone saying his name and he opened his eyes and saw an officer leaning over his cot.

"General, I'm afraid I've come to make trouble for you," the man said.

I'm being arrested, Meade thought. *I wonder why?* Then the man handed Meade a note that said: "You will receive with this the order of the President placing you in command of the Army of the Potomac."

Meade didn't want the job. He actually tried to argue with the officer who brought the message, which was fairly pointless, since the guy was only delivering Lincoln's orders. Meade was taking over an army that had been badly whipped in its last few fights. And now General Lee's army was marching North—another major battle was coming any day.

Soon after Lee's army crossed into Northern territory, a Southern soldier named William Christian wrote a letter home. "My own darling wife," wrote Christian. "We crossed the line day before yesterday and are resting today near a little one-horse town on the road to Gettysburg. Of course we will have to fight here, and when it comes it will be the biggest on record."

He was right.

The Second-Biggest Fourth of July

The Union army followed General Lee's soldiers into Pennsylvania, marching twenty miles a day under a scorching sun. Union men tossed away their extra clothes—it was just too hot to carry heavy backpacks. As they splashed through streams, soldiers took off their dusty shirts and rinsed them quickly and hung them on the tops of their rifles to dry. They marched on with their shirts on their guns, flapping like flags in the summer wind.

Welcome to the North

The good news for Union soldiers was that they were finally back on Northern soil—friendly territory, that is. Citizens came out to cheer and give them food. A nineteen-year-old soldier named Jesse Young remembered marching past a schoolhouse and watching boys and girls pour outside. Waving flowers and flags, the students greeted the weary soldiers with a popular Union song:

"Yes, we'll rally round the flag, boys, we'll rally once again,
Shouting the battle cry of Freedom;
We'll rally from the hillside, we'll gather from the plain,
Shouting the battle cry of Freedom!"

"Many strong men wept as they looked on the scene," Young said.

Southern soldiers got a different greeting—usually curious stares or cold silence. General Lee did have some fans in the North, though. One woman asked for his autograph. Another asked for a lock of his hair. "General Lee said that he really had none to spare," a Southern officer remembered.

Lee's army continued north, capturing supplies, and some soldiers too. James Hodam's regiment captured a very young Union drummer boy. Drummer boys had the important job of sending signals to soldiers by beating rhythms on their drums. Some were twelve or even younger.

Hodam and the boy had this conversation:

Hodam: *Hello, my little Yank. Where are you going?*
Drummer Boy: *Oh, I am a prisoner and am going to Richmond.*
Hodam: *Look here, you are too little to be a prisoner. So pitch that*

drum into that fence-corner, throw off your coat, get behind those bushes, and go home as fast as you can.

Drummer Boy: *Mister, don't you want me for a prisoner?*

Hodam: *No.*

Drummer Boy: *Can I go where I please?*

Hodam: *Yes.*

Drummer Boy: *Then you bet I am going home to Mother!*

The kid tossed away his drum and army coat and dove into the bushes by the side of the road. "I sincerely hope he reached home and Mother," Hodam said.

Let's hope so. The biggest battle ever fought on American soil was about to begin.

Meanwhile, on the Mississippi

But before it does, we've got to check in on the action in the west—events out there were also speeding toward a major turning point.

The scene of the showdown was the Mississippi River. The South still controlled a 140-mile section of the river running through Mississippi and Louisiana. And they were desperate to keep it. If the North gained control of the entire Mississippi River, the Confederacy's land would be sliced in two.

Slicing the Confederacy in two was exactly what General Ulysses S. Grant had in mind. His main problem was the city of Vicksburg, Mississippi, located on steep hills three hundred feet above the Mississippi River. As long as the Confederates held this spot, they could keep control of at least part of the river. Vicksburg, said Jefferson

Davis, "held the South's two halves together."

Grant spent the early months of 1863 trying, and failing, to attack Vicksburg. Actually, his army couldn't even get there—it kept getting stuck in the muddy forests and overgrown swamps around the city. Impatient Northern newspapers were again demanding that Grant be fired.

"I think Grant has hardly a friend left, except myself," Lincoln said. "I propose to stand by him."

Lincoln never regretted that decision. Grant showed that he had something in common with Robert E. Lee—he would take big risks to achieve big goals. In April he marched 40,000 men far to the south of Vicksburg, crossed the river, and headed into Mississippi with only the food his men could carry on their backs.

> *"I was now in the enemy's country, with a vast river and the stronghold* of Vicksburg between me and my base of supplies. But I was on dry ground on the same side of the river with the enemy."*

Ulysses S. Grant

* *a well-defended place*

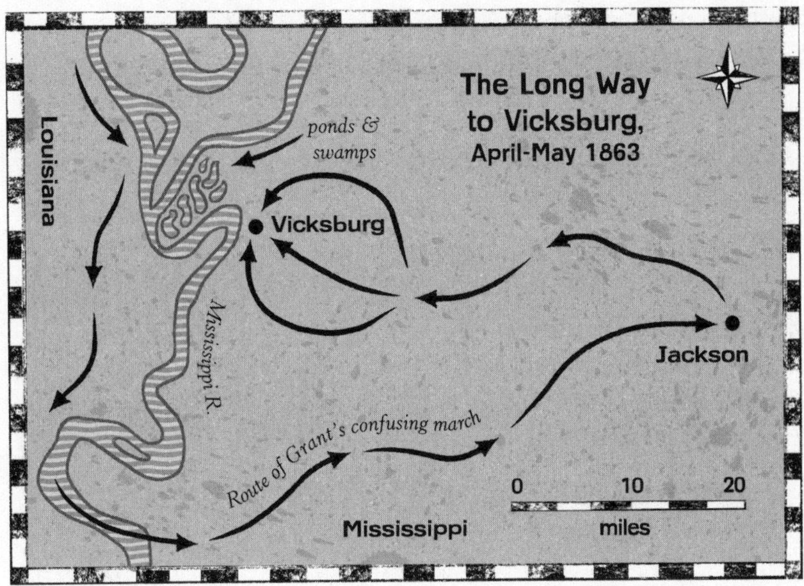

There were about 30,000 Confederate soldiers defending Vicksburg. Instead of heading straight for them, Grant confused everyone (including a very nervous Abe Lincoln) by leading his army east, away from Vicksburg. Moving quickly, keeping Confederate generals guessing, Grant's army zigzagged 180 miles over the next few weeks, winning battles and destroying railroads. Then Grant swung around and headed for Vicksburg—and his plan suddenly became clear. He had been beating or chasing away Confederate forces all over the state. Now the Confederate soldiers in Vicksburg were all alone, cut off from outside help.

Northern newspapers stopped calling Grant a drunken loser. Now he was a hero, even a genius. Lincoln joined the praise, calling Grant "a very determined little fellow."

By the end of May, Grant's army had Vicksburg surrounded. "A cat could not have crept out of Vicksburg without being discovered," said one Confederate soldier. There were still 30,000 Confederate troops in town, though. And they were not about to let Grant come in. Colonel James L. Autry declared: "Mississippians don't know, and refuse to learn, how to surrender to an enemy."

Grant decided to teach them.

They'll Fight All Right

He got some help from the Union army's first African American soldiers. Lincoln's Emancipation Proclamation opened the door for African Americans to enlist in the United States Army. And thousands raced to volunteer.

When a Union general called for black volunteers in New Orleans, a hundred African American shop owners immediately closed their doors and rushed to join the army. These men became part of the First Louisiana Native Guard, the first black regiment in the Union army. The regiment's highest-ranking black officer was Captain André Cailloux, a thirty-eight-year-old cigar factory owner and boxer. One of the youngest volunteers was sixteen-year-old John Crowder, who said he joined the army for two reasons: to serve his country, and to earn money to help his mother.

African American volunteers faced serious prejudice in the army. They were even paid less than white volunteers—starting pay was ten dollars a month for black soldiers, thirteen dollars for white soldiers. (Black soldiers protested this injustice and were finally granted equal pay in 1864.) Many white military leaders and politicians openly doubted that African Americans would succeed as combat soldiers. "Will they fight?" was a question printed in newspapers all over the country.

These new soldiers realized they would be facing more than enemy bullets and bombs. Fair or not, they would be fighting on behalf of all black Americans. In a letter to the Union general Nathaniel Banks, a group of Louisiana volunteers boldly accepted this challenge: "If the world doubts our fighting," they wrote, "give us a chance and we will show them what we can do."

The soldiers got their chance when Union generals decided to attack the Confederate fort at Port Hudson, Louisiana. Along with Vicksburg, this was the last fort on the Mississippi River still in Southern hands. Captain André Cailloux and his men were assigned a leading role in the attack. When he was given the dangerous job of carrying one of the First Louisiana's battle flags, a soldier named Anselmo Planciancios was ready:

"I will bring back these colors in honor, or

report to God the reason why."

Anselmo Planciancios

As soon as the charge toward Port Hudson began, André Cailloux was shot through the left arm. He held his sword high in his right hand and shouted, "Follow me!"—and charged at the guns again.

"They charged and re-charged and didn't know what retreat meant," said a white soldier who fought at Port Hudson.

But the Confederate fort was just too strong. Cailloux was shot again and killed. Planciancios was hit in the head and died instantly. The attack ended in failure as darkness fell.

Though the black soldiers had not captured Port Hudson, their bravery and skill changed minds all over the country. "They fought splendidly," reported General Nathaniel Banks.

Black soldiers soon saw more action when they were attacked at Milliken's Bend, a Union supply post on the Mississippi River. In brutal hand-to-hand fighting with bayonets and rifle butts and fists, they helped defeat the Confederate attack.

Grant was impressed—and convinced he could rely on African American soldiers. And the recent action helped him tighten his grip around the throats of Port Hudson and Vicksburg. Both places started running out of food. A Confederate officer at Port Hudson remembered eating the army mules ("quite tender and juicy"), and then getting even more desperate:

> *"Rats, of which there were plenty about . . . were also caught by many officers and men and were found to be quite a luxury—superior, in the opinion of those who eat them, to spring chicken."*

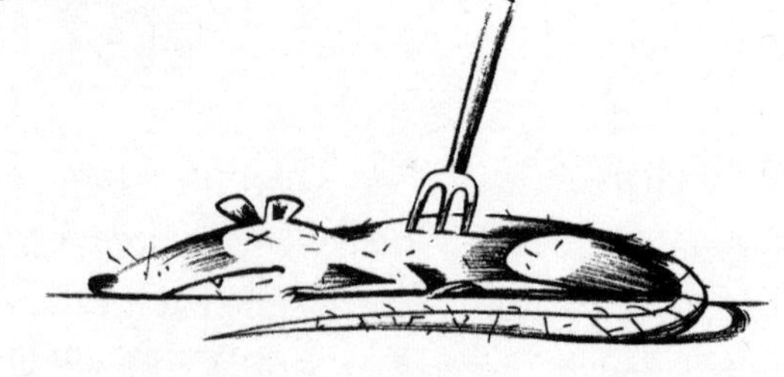

Rats may have tasted good, but they wouldn't last forever.

Where Are Those Shoes?

Now back to Pennsylvania for the battle of Gettysburg.

The whole thing got started when Southern soldiers heard that there was a large supply of shoes in the nearby town of Gettysburg. Thousands of Lee's men were desperate for a new pair of shoes. One barefoot Confederate named John Hancock had tried to make his own sandals out of raw cowhide. He found the results disappointing. "They flop up and down, they stink very bad, and I have to keep a brush in my hand to keep the flies off of them." he said.

On June 30, the Confederate general Henry Heth found his commander, A.P. Hill, and said, "If there is no objection, I will take my division tomorrow and go to Gettysburg and get those shoes."

"None in the world," Hill replied.

So Heth's men set out to find those shoes.

School's Out!

The next day, fifteen-year-old Tillie Pierce was sitting in class at the Young Ladies Seminary of Gettysburg. She and the other students were working on their literature lessons when the teacher suddenly announced: "Children, run home as quickly as you can!"

Everyone jumped up and raced out the door. "Some of the girls did not reach their homes before the rebels were in the streets," Tillie said. "I had scarcely reached the front door, when, on looking up the street, I saw some of the men on horseback. I scrambled in, slammed shut the door, and hastening to the sitting room, peeped out between the shutters."

The Confederate soldiers did not find any shoes in Gettysburg. They did, however, run into a few thousand Union soldiers. No one planned to have a battle here. But when the enemies bumped into each other in town, the men simply did what they had been doing for the past two years—they started fighting, and fighting hard. And that's how the biggest battle of the war began.

When the shooting started, one local farmer looked nervously out at his field. He saw his cow chomping grass on what was about to become a battlefield. "Tell Lee to hold on just a little," he shouted to Southern soldiers, "until I get my cow in out of the pasture." And he ran off to get his cow.

John Burns, another local resident, sat in his house, listening to the gunshots growing louder and louder. This seventy-year-old veteran of the War of 1812 took his ancient musket down from the wall and started cleaning it. His wife wanted to know what he was doing.

"I thought some of the boys might want the old gun," he said.

Then a group of Union soldiers marched past his house, and Burns jumped up and headed for the door.

"Burns, where are you going?" his wife asked.

"I am going out to see what is going on."

And next thing you know, John Burns, wearing his War of 1812 army jacket, was marching into battle with the boys of the Seventh Wisconsin. As they headed into combat, the soldiers gave Burns a new rifle. They offered him an ammunition box, but he said he liked to keep his bullets in his pants pocket.

"I can get my hands in here quicker than in a box. I'm not used to them new-fangled things."

Burns was wounded three times, and when his regiment was driven back he was left lying on the ground. Hours later some kind Confederate soldiers found him and carried him home.

John Burns

Gettysburg: July 1

Meanwhile, a wild day of fighting was raging all over Gettysburg. Neither army had a plan. Robert E. Lee and George Meade were still on their way to town, and neither commander really knew what was going on. But remember, soldiers on both sides had been expecting a big battle. So they figured this must be it. As a Polish-born Union officer named Wlodzimierz Krzyzanowski (his men called him "Kriz") explained: "The fate of the nation was at stake. I felt it, the leaders felt it, the army felt it, and we fought like lions."

As more and more soldiers from both armies reached town, the battle got bigger and bigger. It actually got so loud that people in Pittsburgh, 150 miles away, heard the explosions.

General Lee arrived in Gettysburg that afternoon and studied the situation through his binoculars. He was pleased to see that his army was driving Union forces out of the town

Instead of panicking, though, as they had done in a few previous battles, Union soldiers were gathering in large numbers on the hills just south of town. This was largely thanks to a cool-headed Union general named Winfield Hancock, who took charge on those hills and kept his men calm. "I think this is the strongest position by nature on which to fight a battle that I ever saw," Hancock said.

Lee watched all this through his binoculars as the sun went down. He could see that the Union army was now in a strong position. General James Longstreet, Lee's second-in-command, thought the Confederate army should leave town and find a different place to fight.

"No," said Lee, "the enemy is there, and I am going to attack him there."

"If he is there, it will be because he is anxious that we should attack him," Longstreet argued. "A good reason, in my judgment, for not doing so."

Lee respected Longstreet's opinion (he called Longstreet his "Old War Horse"). But Lee hadn't gotten this far by playing it safe. "They are there in position," Lee said. "And I am going to whip them or they are going to whip me."

The Union commander George Meade finally showed up at about midnight. He met with Hancock and his other generals, who all told him the Union army was in a good spot for tomorrow's fight. "I am glad to hear you say so, gentlemen," Meade said, "for it is too late to leave."

Both armies tried to get some sleep—but everyone was feeling the pressure. "This is the turning point," one Union soldier said to his friend. "If Lee whips us here the Union is lost."

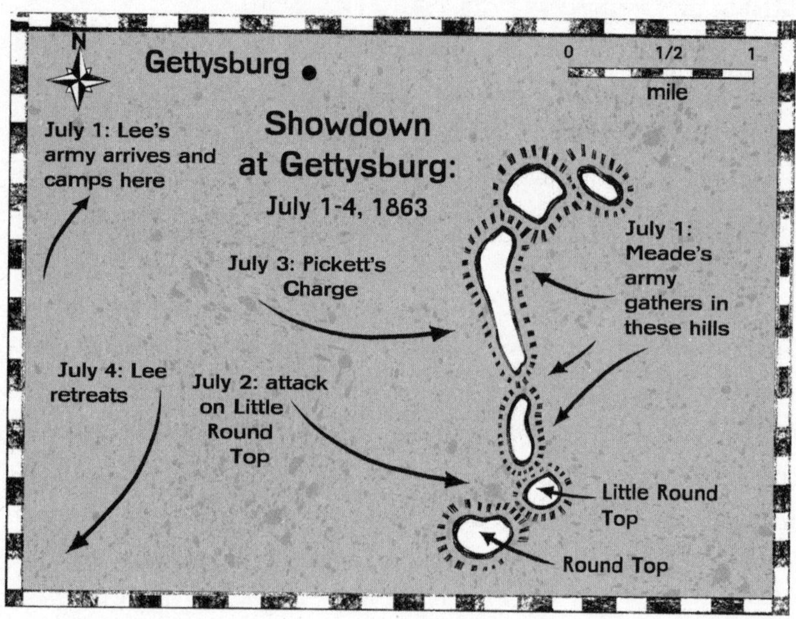

Gettysburg: July 2

The soldiers of the Twentieth Maine Regiment arrived in Gettysburg on the morning of July 2—and they were already exhausted. These men, mainly young fishermen and lumberjacks, had marched more than 125 miles in the past six days. But there was no time to rest.

As soon as they got to Gettysburg, the Twentieth Maine was placed on a rocky, wooded hill called Little Round Top. This was a super-important spot because it was the very left end of the entire Union line. If Union soldiers lost control of this spot, Confederate forces could storm around the end of the Union army and surround it—then capture or kill the whole Union force.

This is exactly what Lee was hoping to do. He ordered a massive attack on the left edge of the Union army.

When the firing started, Colonel Strong Vincent shouted some last-second orders to Joshua Chamberlain, commander of the Twentieth Maine, "This is the left of the Union line. You understand. You are to hold this ground at all costs!"

A year before Chamberlain had been a college professor in Maine. Now he had a very different job—he and his men were to die on this spot rather than retreat or surrender.

Bombs started crashing into the trees on Little Round Top, sending thick branches spinning through the air. Joshua Chamberlain decided his two brothers were standing too close to him. "Boys, I don't like this," he told Tom and John Chamberlain. "Another such shot might make it hard for Mother." The brothers spread out.

Down at the bottom of the hill, Colonel William Oates, commander of the Fifteenth Alabama, was giving his men a moment of rest. These young farmers were just as tired as the Maine men—they had marched twenty-eight miles in the past twelve hours. "Some of my men fainted from the heat, exhaustion, and thirst," Oates remembered. And now it was their job to charge up Little Round Top.

Oates sent a few soldiers off to fill the men's empty canteens. But while waiting for the water, the regiment was ordered to attack immediately. The men desperately needed something to drink—but orders were orders. They started up the hill.

"Look! Look!" shouted the men of the Twentieth Maine when they saw the Alabama soldiers coming up through the trees. This was the start of a ferocious fight in which the soldiers slammed together and drove each other up and down the hill.

"How can I describe the scenes that followed?" wondered Theodore Gerrish of Maine. "Cries, shouts, cheers, groans, prayers, curses, bursting shells, whizzing rifle bullets and clanging steel. . . . The lines at times were so near each other that the hostile gun barrels almost touched."

Both commanders were surrounded by wild fighting and confusion. "At times I saw around me more of the enemy than of my own men," remembered Chamberlain. "My dead and wounded . . . literally covered the ground," Oates said. "The blood stood in puddles in some places on the rocks." Still, he kept leading charge after charge up the hill.

Chamberlain's men were firing so furiously, they ran out of bullets. They grabbed bullets from the wounded and dead, and then ran out of those too. They knew another attack was coming at any minute, and they couldn't just sit there waiting with no ammunition—but they couldn't leave. Chamberlain had an idea. "As a last, desperate resort, I ordered a charge," he said.

"Bayonet!" Chamberlain shouted.

The Maine men attached their bayonets to the ends of their rifles. They jumped up, and with what Theodore Gerrish described as "one wild yell," started running down the hill. "We struck them with a fearful shock," Gerrish said.

The bloodied and exhausted survivors of the Fifteenth Alabama retreated down the hill. The left end of the Union line was safe.

"There never were harder fighters than the Twentieth Maine men and their gallant Colonel. His skill . . . and the great bravery of his men saved Little Round Top and the Army of the Potomac."

William C. Oates

If the men of the Twentieth Maine had lost Little Round Top, the whole history of the war—and the whole history of the United States—might have been different. And for the rest of their lives, the veterans of the Fifteenth Alabama insisted that they would have taken Little Round Top, if only they had been allowed to have a drink of water before going into battle.

Still No Winner

The fight for Little Round Top was just one part of an enormous battle being fought all over Gettysburg on July 2. For General Lee, it was a frustrating day of near misses. His army kept coming close to breaking through the Union army lines, but they just couldn't punch through. For the second day in a row, more than 10,000 soldiers were killed or wounded. And no one had won the battle of Gettysburg yet.

Tillie Pierce, the girl who had run home from school as the fighting began, watched wounded Union soldiers hobbling away from the battlefield.

"The first wounded soldier whom I met had his thumb tied up," she remembered. "This I thought was dreadful, and told him so."

"Oh, this is nothing," he told Tillie. "You'll see worse than this before long."

"Oh! I hope not," she said.

Then the real wounded started coming. "Some limping," Tillie wrote, "some with their heads and arms in bandages, some crawling, others carried on stretchers or brought in ambulances." She went to work, carrying water to the wounded soldiers and tearing up clothing for bandages. And she was amazed at her ability to get used to the sight of operations and amputations and piles of arms and legs—sights she never could have imagined just a few days before.

A twenty-one-year-old teacher named Elizabeth Myers had a similar experience. She nearly fainted when she saw blood flowing from a young soldier's head. "I never could bear the sight of blood," she said. But she decided to stay and help—and she quickly adjusted to the horrible sights. "I was among wounded and dying men day and night," she wrote.

"The soldiers called me brave, but I am afraid the truth was that I did not know enough to be afraid and if I had known enough, I had no time to think of the risk I ran, for my heart and hands were full."

Elizabeth Myers

That night the commanders of both armies met with their top generals. General Lee decided to stay in Gettysburg and try one more attack. "There were never such men in an army before," Lee said of his soldiers. "They will go anywhere and do anything, if properly led."

Across the dark battlefield, General Meade also decided to stay and fight.

Life Under Vicksburg

Meanwhile, down in Mississippi, Grant still had Vicksburg surrounded. His plan was simple: let no food enter Vicksburg, and bomb the city night and day.

"We are utterly cut off from the world, surrounded by a circle of fire," wrote Dora Miller in her diary. "The fiery shower of shells goes on day and night." Miller was one of about three thousand residents trapped in Vicksburg. With bombs crashing through their homes, families scrambled to find new shelter—usually underground.

"Cave-digging has become a regular business," said Miller,

"prices range from twenty to fifty dollars, according to the size of the cave. Two diggers worked at ours for a week and charged thirty dollars."

Many of the caves were dug by enslaved men, who were stuck in town along with everyone else. Families that could afford large caves furnished their new homes with tables, rugs, mirrors, and mattresses. Not that this made life comfortable. "We were almost eaten up by mosquitoes," remembered a young woman named Lida Lord. Then there were the snakes. "A large rattlesnake was found one morning under a mattress on which some of us slept that night," she said.

Snakes were bad, but bombs were worse. Day after day, Mary Loughborough and her family heard shells exploding all around their underground home. "Terror stricken, we remained crouched in the cave," she later wrote. One day a shell actually flew into the cave and crashed into the soft earth inside. The bomb's fuse was sparking and smoking and the family backed helplessly against the dirt walls. "We expected every moment the terrific explosion," Loughborough wrote. Then George, a young slave, snapped into action. "Thus we remained for a moment, with our eyes fixed in terror on the missile of death, when George, the servant boy, rushed forward, seized the shell, and threw it into the street."

"Very thankful was I for our preservation," she said. How did she thank George for saving the family? She didn't say.

The siege of Vicksburg went on and on—twenty days, then thirty, then forty. The food ran out and both soldiers and residents began to starve. Confederate chaplain William Foster described the changing look of soldiers, saying, "The cheeks became thin, the eyes hollow and the flesh began to disappear from the body and limbs."

Hunks of horse and mule meat started showing up in the butcher shops. "Mother would not eat mule meat," remembered a girl named

Lucy McCrae. "But we children ate some, and it tasted right good." When the mules were gone, dogs and cats began disappearing from the streets of Vicksburg.

At the end of June, soldiers in Vicksburg wrote a letter to their commander. "If you can't feed us," they wrote, "you had better surrender, horrible as the idea is."

Gettysburg: July 3

Up in Gettysburg, Robert E. Lee stepped out of his tent a little after three in the morning on July 3. He was already dressed for battle. For the past two days he had been more impatient and restless then anyone had ever seen him.

Lee found his "Old War Horse," General James Longstreet, and told him the plan. They would launch 15,000 soldiers right at the center of the Union army line.

Longstreet didn't like it. "I have been a soldier all my life," he said. "I think I can safely say there never was a body of fifteen thousand men who could make that attack successfully."

But Lee's mind was made up. His army had come so far, fought so hard—all in search of one massive victory that would win the war. Now Lee saw that victory within reach, and he couldn't resist going for it. "The enemy is there," he said, pointing across the battlefield, "and I am going to strike him."

The sun climbed and the temperature soared into the nineties, with high humidity. One soldier from Tennessee called it "the hottest day I think I ever saw."

It was about to get a lot hotter.

Pickett Leads the Charge

Leading the center of Lee's attack was General George Pickett—which explains how this came to be known as "Pickett's Charge." Pickett was known in the army as a fun-loving guy who put perfume on the curls at the end of his long black hair. But today he was deadly serious:

"Up, men, and to your posts!

Don't forget today that you are

from old Virginia!"

The men set out at a steady march across the mile-wide open field separating them from the Union army. "Advance slowly," Confederate officers told their men. "No cheering, no firing."

George Pickett

On the other side of the field, Union soldiers saw what looked like a walking forest of gray uniforms and guns and battle flags—all moving right at them. "No man who looked on the scene can ever forget it," the Union soldier Jesse Young said. It was terrifying, but it was also exciting. Union soldiers knew they had the advantage. They were on a low hill, lying behind stone walls and mounds of dirt. All they had to do was wait until the enemy was within range and then start blasting.

"Steady, boys," Union officers cautioned. "Hold your position, don't fire until the word is given, keep cool, lie low till order is given to fire, make ready, take good aim."

One Northern soldier realized he hadn't eaten anything all day. Then he decided he was glad, since his empty stomach allowed him to lie flatter on the ground.

"Come on, Johnny! Keep coming!" Union soldiers shouted.

They did keep coming—and then the Union rifles and cannons opened fire. "Arms, heads, blankets, guns, and knapsacks were tossed into the clear air," a Union officer later said.

"At every step some poor fellow would fall, and his pitiful cry would come to my ear," remembered John James, a Virginia soldier. And still the Confederate charge continued.

Some of the attackers fought their way up to the Union's stone walls, but they were quickly blasted back. The attack was shattered. More than half of the soldiers who set out on Pickett's Charge did not return. (Pickett survived, though he never forgave Lee for sending him on the doomed charge.)

General Lee watched survivors staggering back toward the Confederate lines. He rode back and forth, trying to encourage his men. "It's all my fault," he told them. "All this has been my fault. It is I that have lost this fight, and you must help me out of it the best you can."

Union soldiers, meanwhile, watched Lee's soldiers retreat—something they had not seen much of so far. This was a cause for celebration. "Some cried, others shook hands," one Union soldier remembered, "and all joined in the best cheer we could get up."

The Second-Biggest Fourth of July

The next day, July 4, 1863, has to rank as the second most important Fourth of July in U.S. history. (July 4, 1776—the day Congress approved the Declaration of Independence—is still number one.) Two things made July 4, 1863, huge. First, General Lee faced the harsh truth that he had been beaten at Gettysburg, that his invasion of the North had failed. And, in a pounding rainstorm, Lee's battered army began the long retreat back to Virginia.

Second, after suffering through a forty-seven-day siege, the Confederate army at Vicksburg finally surrendered to General Grant. "We are now in the darkest hour of our political existence," moaned Jefferson Davis. When Abraham Lincoln heard the news, he leaped from his chair and threw his long arm around the secretary of the navy, Gideon Welles, and shouted:

"I cannot, in words, tell you my joy over this result. It is great, Mr. Welles, it is great!"

Abraham Lincoln

The Confederates surrendered Port Hudson a few days later, giving the Union control of the entire Mississippi River. Now, for the first time, Lincoln believed the end of the war was in sight. "Peace does not appear so distant as it did," he said. General Meade just had to chase down Lee's badly wounded army and capture it—and that would be the end of the Confederate States of America.

But when did things ever go right for Abraham Lincoln?

Can Anyone Win This War?

Was the South ready to quit fighting after those painful losses at Gettysburg and Vicksburg? Not even close. Southern spirit was still strong—as you can see from these questions in a math textbook used by Southern students during the war:

> 1. *A Confederate soldier captured eight Yankees each day for nine days. How many Yankees did he capture in all?*
> 2. *If one Confederate soldier can whip seven Yankees, how many Confederate soldiers can whip forty-nine Yankees?*

No, the South was nowhere near ready to give up.

They're Getting Away!

Today we think of the Union victories at Gettysburg and Vicksburg as the major turning point of the Civil War. After these battles the South would never again be strong enough to invade the North. But in July of 1863, Abraham Lincoln had no way of knowing this. In July of 1863, these Union victories were just another reason for Lincoln to get depressed.

You'll recall that the Union army under General George Meade had just beaten Robert E. Lee's army at Gettysburg. Now Lee's army—what was left of it—was limping home like a wounded animal. If Lee could get safely back to Virginia, his army would have time to rest and recover. But if Meade attacked right away, he might be able to crush Lee once and for all.

Meade was cautious by nature, though. Plus, his army was still exhausted from the three-day Gettysburg fight. Lincoln urged Meade to get on with the attack. But this only annoyed Meade; it didn't make him move. (Meade was so easily annoyed that soldiers called him "Old Snapping Turtle.")

Lincoln spent the next few days looking over maps, pacing impatiently, longing for news. Finally, on July 12, Meade declared that he was nearly ready to attack. Too late—the next night, Lee's army escaped across the Potomac River into Virginia. Lincoln was sick with disappointment. "We had them in our grasp." he said. "We had only to stretch forth our hands and they were ours. And nothing I could say or do could make the army move."

Now there was no end in sight. Just the thought of how much work lay ahead made Lincoln drop his head onto his desk and shut his eyes. "I'm a tired man," he groaned. "Sometimes I'm the tiredest man on earth."

We've All Got Troubles

Robert E. Lee's soldiers might disagree. In their rush to escape from Gettysburg, they marched night and day through sticky mud and nonstop rain. "For ninety-six hours we were almost constantly on our feet," one soldier remembered. "There was no time to cook rations and the boys went on about two biscuits and no meat a day."

"The whole of the army was dozing while marching," another soldier said.

And those were the lucky ones. The unlucky ones were the wounded, who were loaded into wagons that bounced and rattled over rough roads. The wounded men suffered unbearable pain as their blood-soaked clothes dried, hardened, and poked into their open wounds. Horrible cries were heard coming from these wagons.

"Will no one have mercy and kill me?" shouted one wounded soldier.

Another yelled: "Stop! Oh! For God's sake, stop just for one minute; take me out and leave me to die on the roadside!"

General Lee himself was exhausted, sick, and desperately in need of some time off. Once back in Virginia, he actually wrote to Jefferson Davis suggesting that Davis find a new commander for the army. "I sensibly feel the growing failure of my bodily strength," Lee told Davis. "I cannot even accomplish what I myself desire. How can I fulfill the expectations of others?"

Davis refused to even consider this request. "Our country could not bear to lose you," Davis wrote to Lee. "Take all possible care of yourself."

But who was going to take care of Davis? The war was going badly, and the never-ending stress was making his headaches worse—causing explosions of pain in his face and blinding his left eye. Southern newspapers and members of Congress blamed Davis for everything that was going wrong. (And they were pretty cruel too: one Southern leader called Davis "miserable, stupid" and "one-eyed.")

When they weren't insulting Davis, many members of the Confederate Congress were busy attacking each other—and I do mean attacking. During one heated debate, Senator Benjamin Hill threw an ink bottle at Senator William Yancey, ripping open Yancey's cheek. Henry Foote was known to assault fellow members of Congress with a variety of weapons, including a pistol, a knife, and an umbrella.

And there was more bad news for Jefferson Davis. The women of Richmond were rioting!

Riots in the South

The cause of the riot was simple: many families were starving. Two years of roaring battles had destroyed farms throughout the South. And there was very little money to buy imported food, because Southern farmers were unable to export their cotton to Europe. Europeans wanted to buy the cotton, but Southern ships couldn't get it there—Union warships were blockading almost every Southern port.

As a result, fresh food was scarce. The prices of basic items such as flour, corn, and meat were rising out of control. When a woman walked into a store in Richmond and asked the price of a barrel of flour, the merchant demanded seventy dollars. That led to this exchange:

Woman: *My God! How can I pay such prices? I have seven children; what shall I do?*
Merchant: *I don't know madam, unless you eat your children.*

The soaring cost of food sparked riots in more than a dozen Southern cities. In Atlanta, women with knives and guns entered shops and asked the price of goods they needed. If they felt the prices were unfairly high, they simply took the food home to their families.

In Richmond, a thirty-seven-year-old mother of four named Mary Jackson led the largest of these "bread riots." The Richmond Bread Riot began when a crowd of several hundred women surrounded Jackson, cheering her demands for fair prices. Then they followed her through the streets, smashing store windows, grabbing goods, and chanting, "Bread! Bread! Bread!"

"Some had hatchets and axes," one witness said. "Some clubs, some knives, and many carried bayonets in their belts."

When asked why she had joined the angry mob, an eighteen-year-old woman explained:

"We are starving. We are going to the bakeries and each of us will take a loaf of bread. That is little enough for the government to give us after it has taken all our men."

Jefferson Davis ran out into the street, jumped onto a wagon, and told the rioters to go home. The people responded with boos and hisses. Davis pulled some coins from his pockets and threw them to the crowd. "Here is all I have," he told them. "It is not much, but take it!" This didn't seem to help.

Then Davis got serious. In five minutes, he warned, soldiers would begin firing at the crowd. He pulled out his pocket watch and counted off one minute, then two, three, four . . . No one moved.

Davis held up the watch and shouted:

"My friends, you have one minute more!"

That did it—the people went home, muttering and still hungry.

Meanwhile, up North, a much more serious riot was about to explode.

Riots in the North

On the morning of July 13, 1863, Martha Perry was sitting in her New York City apartment when she was startled by a burst of noise in the street below. "I heard loud and continued cheers," she later wrote, "and supposed it must be news of some great victory."

She quickly realized how wrong she was. "I flew to my window," she said, "and saw rushing up Lexington Avenue, within a few paces of our house, a great mob of men, women and children. The men, in red working shirts, looking fairly fiendish as they brandished clubs, threw stones, and fired pistols. Many of the women had babies in their arms, and all of them were completely lawless as they swept on."

This was the start of the New York City Draft Riots—the biggest and most violent riots in the history of the United States.

The trouble had begun in March 1863, when the government announced that it would begin drafting men into the Union army. This sparked anger for many reasons. Plenty of people were already sick of war and simply did not want to get shot at. Many were also furious about an incredibly bogus part of the draft law. If you were drafted, the law said, you could get out of serving by paying the government three hundred dollars. This was easy for a rich man to do, but it took the average worker about a year to earn three hundred dollars! This led to a protest cry: "A rich man's war and a poor man's fight!"

There was another, uglier reason for the draft protests—racial prejudice. Since Lincoln's Emancipation Proclamation, people realized that the North was fighting to preserve the Union and to end slavery. Many white workers wondered, Why should we risk our lives to help African Americans? Freed slaves will just come to the North and compete with us for jobs.

When the draft began in New York City, furious workers marched to the government office where the draft was taking place. Inside the office, a blindfolded government worker was quietly drafting soldiers by pulling names from a large spinning wheel. Outside, a mob was shouting and waving clubs and pulling up bricks and stones from the street. Then the anger erupted as the mob smashed the office windows, charged inside, and started destroying everything in sight.

The draft riots raged out of control for the next three days. Mobs of thousands attacked and burned government offices, police stations, and newspapers that supported President Lincoln. The city glowed red at night as fires burned everywhere and rioters chanted:

"No draft!"

"The poor man's blood for the rich man's money!"

"Tell Old Abe to come to New York!"

Rioters attacked policemen, anyone who looked rich, and African Americans. Several black men were beaten to death. One mob even attacked an orphanage for African American children. Two hundred children escaped out the back as the cursing crowd set fire to the building.

Union soldiers rushed to New York from the battle of Gettysburg and finally ended the riots—by firing into the raging crowds. More than a hundred people were killed in the draft riots.

Down in Washington, Abraham Lincoln said he felt as if he were sitting on a volcano.

General Tubman in Action

But this was a wild and massive war, and sometimes bad news and good news came at the same time. If Abe Lincoln had picked up a Boston newspaper called *The Commonwealth* on July 10, 1863, he would have read a story that began with this remarkable sentence: "Colonel Montgomery and his gallant band of 300 black soldiers, under the guidance of a black woman, dashed into the enemy's country, struck a bold and effective blow . . . without losing a man or receiving a scratch."

The black woman in question was Harriet Tubman, the former Underground Railroad hero—known to her admirers as "General Tubman."

When the Civil War began, Tubman went to work for the Union army as a cook and nurse. She didn't stop there. While working with the army in South Carolina, Tubman boldly slipped into Confederate territory, gathering information from slaves she met and studying the local geography. Then she came up with a plan.

On the night of June 2, 1863, three Union gunships cruised up the Combahee River. Aboard the ships were the black soldiers of the Second South Carolina Regiment. Guiding the lead boat was Harriet Tubman.

Tubman knew exactly where to find warehouses piled high with cotton and rice. Union soldiers jumped off the boats, setting fire to the warehouses and taking the opportunity to torch the homes of plantation owners as well. At the same time, entire families of escaping slaves raced to the riverbank and leaped to freedom on the Union boats. "I never saw such a sight," Tubman said.

"Women would come with twins hanging around their necks . . . bags on their shoulders, baskets on their heads, and young ones tagging along behind, all loaded; pigs squealing, chickens screaming, young ones squealing."

Harriet Tubman

Tubman's Combahee River raid was a smashing success. Union soldiers destroyed tons of supplies that the South badly needed. And about 750 men, women, and children escaped from slavery on nearby plantations. More than one hundred of the men quickly joined the Union army.

The only flaw in her plan, Tubman later said, was her choice in clothing. In the rush to escape, people (and animals) kept stepping on and ripping the end of her dress. "I made up my mind then I would never wear a long dress on another expedition of the kind," Tubman said.

Soldiers for the Cause

While escaped slaves were joining the Union army in the South, African Americans in the North were also signing up to fight. In early 1863 the Fifty-fourth Massachusetts became the first African American regiment raised in the North.

"Every black man and woman feels a special interest in the success of this regiment," declared a newspaper called the *Anglo-African*. The abolitionist leader Frederick Douglass certainly had a special interest—his sons Lewis and Charles enlisted in the Fifty-fourth Massachusetts.

The soldiers of this new regiment made national headlines in July 1863 when they led an attack on Fort Wagner, a strong Confederate fort on an island in Charleston Harbor, South Carolina. Here's what happened.

Just before dark on July 18, the men of the Fifty-fourth Massachusetts began marching through the sand leading up to Fort Wagner's walls and guns. The beach was narrow, and some of the soldiers were splashing through ocean water up to their waists. Then the fort's guns exploded with what Lewis Douglass described as "a perfect hail" of bullets and bombs. "Men fell all around me," Douglass remembered. "How I got out of that fight alive I cannot tell."

The Union soldiers charged the last hundred yards up to the fort's walls. When twenty-three-year-old Sergeant William Carney reached the wall, he saw the soldier who was carrying the American flag go down. Carney grabbed the flag and pounced up the sloping fort wall. He was soon shot in the leg, but he stayed up there, waving the stars and stripes. "In this position I remained quite a while," he said.

When the surviving members of the Fifty-fourth Massachusetts were finally forced to retreat, Carney was hit four more times—in the chest, the right arm, and again in the right leg, and a final bullet grazed his head. Somehow still holding the flag, Carney called to his fellow fighters: "Let us go back to the fort!"

"And the officer in charge said, 'Sergeant, you have done enough; you are badly wounded . . .' when I replied, 'I have only done my duty, the old flag never touched the ground.'"

William Carney

For his actions at Fort Wagner, Carney became the first African American to be awarded the Medal of Honor, the nation's highest military honor.

The skill and bravery of the Fifty-fourth Massachusetts finally silenced the people who were still claiming that African Americans would not make good soldiers. And black men continued joining the army—more than 200,000 served in the Union forces by the end of the war.

"This year has brought about many changes that at the beginning were or would have been thought impossible," wrote Christopher Fleetwood at the end of 1863. "The close of the year finds me a soldier for the cause of my race. May God bless the cause, and enable me in the coming year to forward it on."

A Few Words at Gettysburg

In the fall of 1863, Abraham Lincoln got his own chance to talk about the cause for which he was fighting. A cemetery dedicated to the Union soldiers who had died in the battle of Gettysburg was about to be opened, and Lincoln was invited say a few words at the opening ceremony. So he took a train to Gettysburg and said a few words—and they turned out to be some of the most famous words in American history.

In the Gettysburg Address, Lincoln spoke of the big goals the Union was fighting for, like democracy and freedom and—well, let's just listen to the speech.

"Fourscore and seven years ago our fathers brought forth upon this continent a new nation, conceived in liberty and dedicated to the proposition that all men are created equal.

Now we are engaged in a great civil war, testing whether that nation or any nation so conceived and so dedicated can long endure. We are met on a great battlefield of that war. We have come to dedicate a portion of that field as a final resting-place for those who here gave their lives that that nation might live. It is altogether fitting and proper that we should do this.

But, in a larger sense, we cannot dedicate, we cannot consecrate, we cannot hallow this ground. The brave men, living and dead, who struggled here have consecrated it far above our poor power to add or detract. The world will little note nor long remember what we say here, but it can never forget what they did here. It is for us the living, rather, to be dedicated here to the unfinished work which they who fought here have thus far so nobly advanced. It is rather for us to be here dedicated to the great task remaining before us—that from these honored dead we take increased devotion to that cause for which they gave the last full measure of devotion—that we here highly resolve that these dead shall not have died in vain—that this nation, under God, shall have a new birth of freedom, and that government of the people, by the people, for the people, shall not perish from the earth."

Abraham Lincoln's Gettysburg Address lasted just two minutes. A photographer was racing to set up his camera (which took a long time in those days). By the time he was ready, Lincoln had finished speaking and was back in his chair. After sitting down, Lincoln turned to his bodyguard Ward Lamon. "Lamon," he said, "that speech . . .

is a flat failure and the people are disappointed." Many newspapers agreed, calling Lincoln's words "silly" and "flat" and "dull."

But over the years people have come to appreciate the power and beauty of the Gettysburg Address. In ten carefully crafted sentences, Lincoln presented a bold dream for the future of the United States—and for people everywhere. Union soldiers, he said, were fighting for the ideals of freedom and democracy. By winning this war, the Union would prove that democratic government could work. And as a result, freedom would continue to expand, both at home and all over the world.

The night after his speech, Lincoln rode the train back to Washington. Too tired for conversation, he stretched out across several seats with a wet towel over his face. He had explained as clearly as he could what he believed the Union was fighting for. But he had no idea if the Union could actually win.

10,000 Battles

There were more than 10,000 large and small battles in the Civil War. Now we will review all of them.

Well, maybe not. But we do need to check in on two big fights from late 1863—battles that helped answer Lincoln's question about whether or not the Union could win this war.

Let's begin at Chickamauga Creek in Georgia. In September about 60,000 Confederate soldiers led by General Braxton Bragg attacked 60,000 Union soldiers under General William Rosecrans. Bragg's forces smashed through the Union lines, sending thousands of Union troops—including General Rosecrans—sprinting from the battlefield.

"They have fought their last man, and he is running!" shouted the Confederate general James Longstreet.

Not all the Union soldiers were running away, though. The Union general George Thomas kept thousands of men on the battlefield, fighting until dark. One of the Union "men" who stayed and fought was a twelve-year-old drummer boy named Johnny Clem.

Two years earlier, Johnny had left his home in Ohio and tried to join the Third Ohio Regiment. But the commander, Johnny remembered, "said he wasn't enlisting infants." Johnny kept trying, and was finally taken on as a drummer boy by a Michigan regiment.

"He was an expert drummer," said Johnny's sister. "And being a bright, cheery child, soon made his way into the affections of officers and soldiers."

Johnny may have been "cheery," but when a bomb destroyed his drum at the battle of Shiloh, he got pretty angry.

"I did not like to stand and be shot at without shooting back."

So the soldiers gave Johnny his own rifle—first sawing off the end of the barrel to make it lighter. And he had this gun with him at the battle of Chickamauga. At one point in the battle, a Confederate officer rode up to him and shouted: "Surrender, you little Yankee!"

Johnny shot the man off his horse and escaped.

The two-day battle of Chickamauga turned into the second-bloodiest battle

Johnny Clem

of the war—second only to Gettysburg. Southern soldiers fought their way to a victory that improved the mood of the entire Confederacy. John Jones, who worked for the Confederate government in Richmond, noticed an immediate change on the faces of people in the streets. "This announcement has lifted a heavy load from the spirits of our people," Jones wrote in his diary. "The effects of this great victory will be electrical."

General Rosecrans's army, meanwhile, retreated north to Chattanooga, Tennessee. Southern forces began surrounding the city.

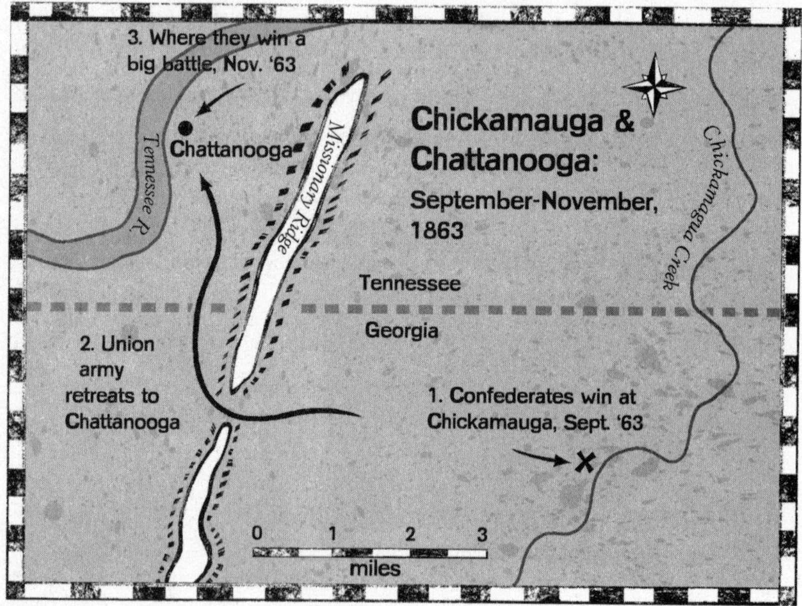

Helps to Be Lucky

Rosecrans had been a pretty good general so far, but now he seemed unable to recover from the shock of Chickamauga. As Abraham Lincoln put it, Rosecrans appeared "confused and stunned like a duck hit on the head." Since this was not a quality Lincoln was looking for his military leaders, he sent in a general he trusted more: Ulysses S. Grant. By late November, Grant was ready to attack. And his attack worked, though not quite according to plan.

Part of Grant's plan at the battle of Chattanooga was to have some of his soldiers march to the bottom of a steep hill called Missionary Ridge. But they were not supposed to charge up the hill—there were way too many Confederate soldiers and guns up there.

Chomping on a cigar, Grant watched the action through binoculars from a nearby hilltop. He saw Union troops fight their way to the base of Missionary Ridge. Then he saw something alarming: the soldiers were charging up the hill! Grant turned angrily to the generals George Thomas and Gordon Granger:

Grant: *Thomas, who ordered those men up the ridge?*
Thomas: *I don't know. I did not. Did you order them up, Granger?*
Granger: *No, they started up without orders. When those fellows get started all *#$%! can't stop them.*

Grant bit down on his cigar. "Someone will suffer for it," he muttered, "if it turns out badly."

This was a perfect example of how little control generals had over Civil War battles. Once the shooting started, they really had no idea what was going to happen. At Chattanooga, Grant got lucky. Union soldiers swept up Missionary Ridge, driving off General Bragg's Confederate forces and charging their way to a huge Union victory.

Southerners, who had been so happy after Chickamauga, were now depressed again. In Richmond, John Jones noted that the bad news put his children in a kind of daze. "Bragg's disaster so shocked my son Custis," he said, "that, at dinner, when asked for rice, he poured water into his sister's plate."

An even more significant effect of this battle was that Abraham Lincoln decided to put Grant in charge of the entire Union army. Grant set off for Washington to make plans with Lincoln. And to meet him—the Union's two most important leaders had never seen each other in person.

Miserable Prison Camps

Not all Union soldiers were as lucky as General Grant. John Ransom, a twenty-year-old soldier from Michigan, was taken prisoner during the fighting in Tennessee. He was shipped to Georgia, where he found himself in Andersonville—the most dreaded prisoner of war camp in the South.

Andersonville was simply a large open field surrounded by wooden walls, designed to hold 10,000 prisoners. But by the summer of 1864, more than 30,000 Union soldiers were crowded into the camp. With no place to hide from the sizzling sun, prisoners baked in the filthy open field.

"My heart aches for the poor wretches, Yankees though they are," said a Georgia woman named Eliza Andrews.

The entire South was short of food, so Union prisoners suffered from hunger along with everyone else. And at Andersonville the only water for drinking and bathing (and using as a toilet) was a thin stream winding though the open field. Ransom wrote in his diary:

"Nothing can be worse or nastier than the stream drizzling its way through this camp. . . . Dead bodies lay around all day in the broiling sun, by the dozen and even hundreds. . . . It's too horrible for me to describe in fitting language."

John Ransom

Disease and hunger killed quickly in Andersonville—an average of nearly thirty prisoners died every day. Ransom wrote in his diary that it was taking every ounce of energy and willpower he had just to stay alive: "Could die in two hours if I wanted to, but don't."

Meanwhile, Southern prisoners were just as miserable in Northern prison camps. A Tennessee soldier named Marcus Toney shivered through a bitter winter at the Elmira prison camp in New York. Even as temperatures dropped to twenty degrees below zero, prisoners were not given enough warm clothing or blankets. In a hopeless attempt to get warm, four men crowded into each wooden bunk. Everyone had to sleep on his side, Toney remembered, and no one could move on his own: "When ready to change positions, one would call out, 'All turn to the right'; and the next call would be, 'All turn to the left.' The turns had to be made as stated, or there would be collisions."

A group of Alabama prisoners decided to bust out of Elmira the only way possible—by going underground. Beginning inside their tent, they dug down six feet, then started tunneling toward the prison walls, sixty-eight feet away.

"We thought we could dig our way out in four or five days," John Maull remembered, "but soon discovered it was no easy task."

Knowing that the prison guards would hear any shoveling noises, they dug silently with pocketknives—that slowed things down a bit. Then they ran into two problems that have faced everyone who has ever tried to dig an escape tunnel. First, the lack of oxygen in the narrow tunnel gave them dizzy spells and headaches. Second, they somehow had to get rid of all the dirt they were digging up. Their solution was to stuff the dirt into their pockets and stroll around the camp at night, scattering it casually, little by little.

After about two months of work, the diggers hit the underground base of the prison wall. The men dug a little deeper and went under the wall. Then they dug their way up, broke through the surface, and looked up at a bright moon.

"Half past three o'clock and all is well!" they heard a guard inside the camp shout.

Ten men made it out of Elmira that night. They grabbed some corn and apples from a nearby farm, then split up. Amazingly, nine of them made it safely back to the South.

But tens of thousands of soldiers were still suffering in prison camps, North and South. And they knew they would probably be stuck there until the end of the war. When would that be?

Ulysses S. Grant was thinking about that same question.

U.S. Grant and Son

A clerk stood behind the front desk of Willard's Hotel in Washington, D.C. It was a late afternoon in March 1864.

The clerk looked up and watched a man and a boy approach the desk. The man was wearing a sloppy and dirty military uniform—the uniform of a general in the Union army. But so what? Generals came and went from Willard's all the time.

The man asked for a room. The clerk said he might have something, perhaps a small room on the top floor.

That would be fine, the man said.

The clerk pointed to the registration book. The man turned the book toward him and signed: "U.S. Grant and son."

The clerk's eyes nearly popped out of his head when he read his guest's name. Suddenly becoming very respectful, he insisted that Grant take the best suite of rooms in the hotel.

After checking in, Grant and his fourteen-year-old son, Fred, went to the dining room. As usual, Grant was feeling shy and hoping no one would notice him. But other diners were looking over and whispering and pointing. Then a man sitting nearby started pounding his knife on the table. He shouted: "I have the honor to inform you that General Grant is present in the room with us!"

Everyone jumped up and started chanting: "Grant! Grant! Grant!"

Grant stood and made an awkward bow. Then he sat down and tried to finish his meal. A newspaper reporter described the general as "blushing and confused."

How could it get worse? That evening, Grant was invited to a party at the White House. As soon as he walked into the East Room, he was mobbed by men and women in fancy evening wear. Then Grant saw a very tall man working his way through the crowd—a man he recognized from pictures he'd seen.

"It is General Grant, is it not?" asked Abraham Lincoln.

"Yes," Grant replied.

"I'm glad to see you, General."

And they shook hands.

Next, Grant was paraded around the room, arm in arm with Mary Lincoln. People jumped onto chairs and tables to get a better view.

Someone shouted: "Stand up so we can all have a look at you!"

But Grant was standing—he just wasn't that tall. So people made him step up onto a sofa. And Grant stood up there for a while, beet red and sweating rivers, and mumbling something about wanting to be "left alone."

In a brief ceremony a couple days later, Grant was officially placed in charge of all Union forces. Lincoln asked him to stay in town for a dinner in his honor. But Grant politely declined—at this point he just wanted to get back to the war.

"Really, Mr. Lincoln," Grant said, "I have had enough of this show business."

We Must Whip Them!

A few weeks later, down in Richmond, Varina Davis walked from her home to her husband's office, carrying Jefferson's lunch on a tray. Jefferson Davis was just sitting down to eat when he heard a servant let loose a terrible scream.

The news was awful: Jefferson and Varina's five-year-old son, Joe, had just slipped off a balcony, falling thirty feet to the brick ground below. Joe died moments later.

Davis tried to go back to work, but it was useless. He threw down the papers he was supposed to read, crying, "I must have this day with my little son!"

Like Lincoln two years before, Davis had lost a child. And like Lincoln, Davis had very little time to grieve. Another year of fighting was about to begin, and the South needed a plan.

As always, Robert E. Lee was itching to attack, and he had something to tell his officers:

"We have got to whip them! We must whip them!"

Ulysses S. Grant ***Robert E. Lee***

But Lee and Davis agreed that risking a major attack was not the best strategy for the South at that moment. The Union was going to have a presidential election in November—and this was the key to the South's strategy. Lincoln was running for reelection, but he was looking pretty weak. People up north were sick of the endless bloodshed and were longing for peace. So it was very possible that voters might elect a new president, one who was willing to end the war by giving the South its independence.

The next six months were everything. The Confederate army had to make it through the next six months without losing any major battles. That way, when it was time for the election in November, the end of the war would still be nowhere in sight. Northern voters would blame Lincoln for this—and they would boot him out of office.

All of this brought up an important question: Would Union war strategy change now that Grant was in charge of Union forces? Definitely, said the Confederate general James Longstreet. A college friend of Grant's (and a guest at his wedding), Longstreet had followed Grant's career closely. And he warned his fellow officers to prepare for nonstop action: "That man will fight us every day and every hour till the end of the war."

That's exactly what Grant was planning to do.

The Bloody Road to Richmond

What is it like to march into your own nightmare? Union soldiers found out in May 1864, as they moved south into the dark and tangled Virginia forest known as the Wilderness. The year before in this place they had been whipped in the battle of Chancellorsville. Now they were marching past the remains of soldiers killed in that fight: twisted skeletons and white skulls that seemed to be staring up at them. Union soldiers knew they were about to face another big battle in these spooky woods—and they had a bad, bad feeling about it.

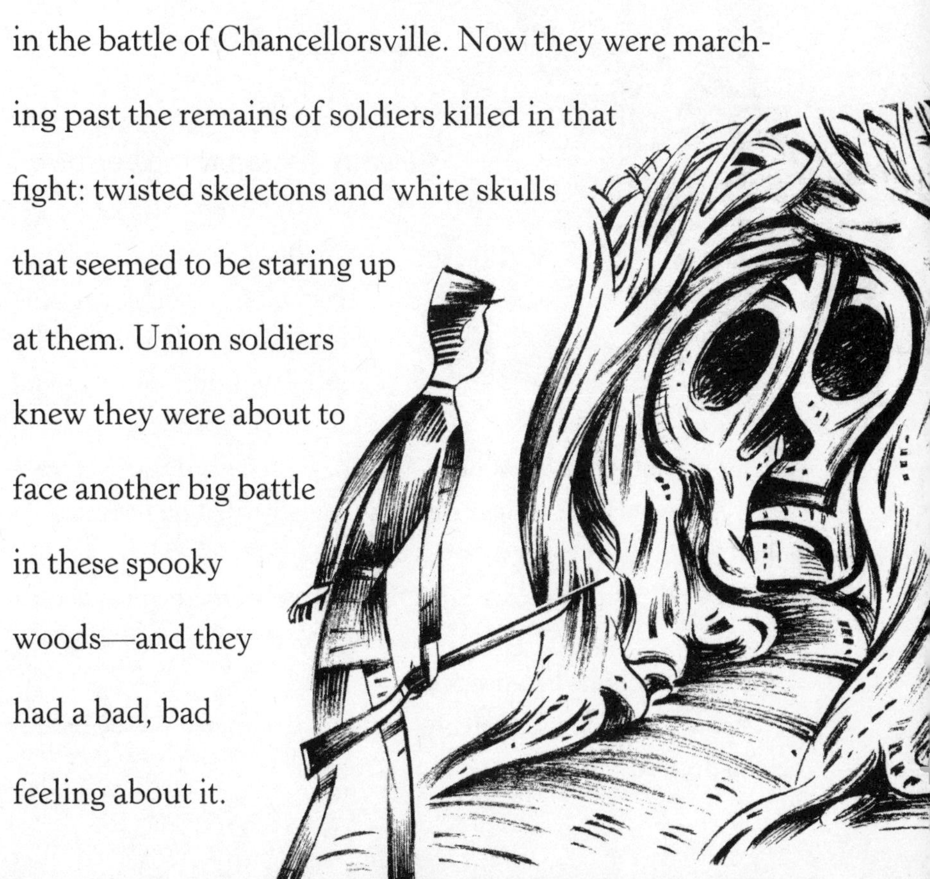

Grant's Pretty Simple Plan

In the spring of 1864 there were two main Confederate armies. One was in Virginia, under the command of Robert E. Lee. The other, in Georgia, was led by Joseph Johnston. Grant decided to attack both of these armies at the same time.

The Union general William Tecumseh Sherman described Grant's plan like this:

"He was to go for Lee and I was to go for Joe Johnston. That was his plan."

William Tecumseh Sherman

Okay, so it wasn't a fancy plan. But Grant knew that he and Sherman had twice as many soldiers as Lee and Johnston. Grant's strategy was to use this advantage to "hammer continuously against the armed force of the enemy." He was convinced that the larger Union forces could pound their way to victory.

But could Union forces win a big victory before the presidential election in November? If not, Lincoln was going to lose—and the South would gain its independence.

The future of the United States would be decided on the battlefield in the next few months.

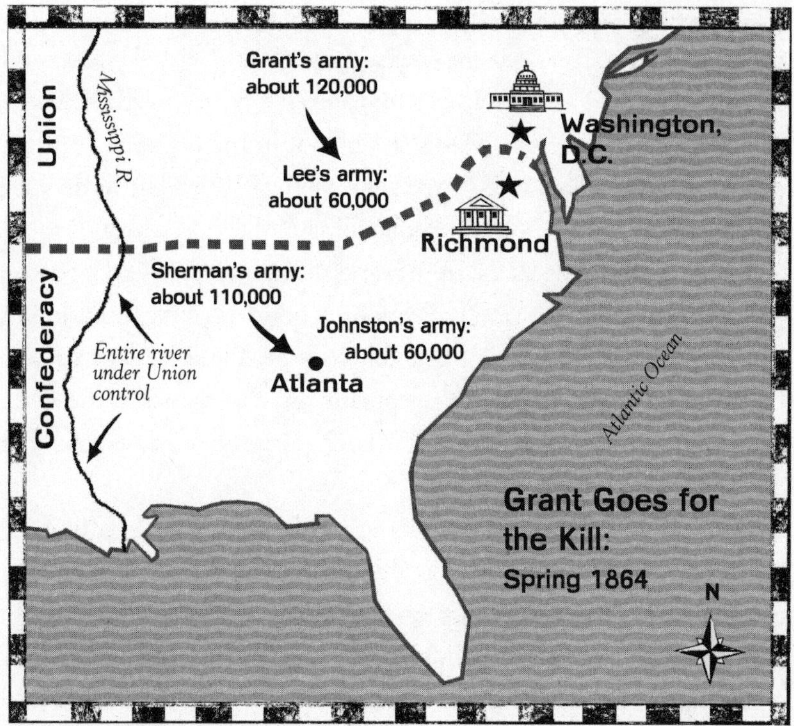

Once More into the Wilderness

That explains why Grant stuffed so many cigars into the pockets of his pants and jacket before leaving his tent each morning—chewing and smoking cigars helped him handle the terrible pressure he was under.

Grant began his part of the plan by leading his army south into Virginia in early May 1864. While Union troops were tripping through the heavily wooded Wilderness, Lee's army attacked. This sparked one of the war's most confusing battles—and that's saying something.

"No one could see the fight fifty feet from him," said the Union soldier Warren Goss. "It was a blind and bloody hunt to the death."

Men on both sides were ordered to charge at the enemy. Slight problem: no one could see the enemy through the twisted bushes and vines and trees. The only way to find the enemy was to stumble forward and crash into him. After being shot in the leg and captured, one Texas soldier shouted, "You Yanks don't call this a battle, do you? Our two armies ain't nothing but howling mobs!"

Thorns ripped soldiers' clothes and sliced their skin as they drove each other through the woods. Exploding bombs set trees on fire, and the wind blew smoke and unbearable heat back and forth across the battlefield. "The men fought the enemy and the flames at the same time," Warren Goss remembered. "Their hair and beards were singed and their faces blistered."

Grant spent most of the battle of the Wilderness sitting on a log, listening to reports from his officers and puffing cigars so furiously that his head disappeared in a cloud of yellow smoke. He went through twenty cigars in one day (a personal record), and with good reason—like every other Union general who had marched into Virginia, Grant was taking a whipping from Robert E. Lee. Grant's forces suffered more than 17,000 casualties in the Wilderness, compared to about 8,000 for Lee's army.

Grant was off to a terrible start.

No Turning Back

When the Wilderness fighting ended, Grant walked into his tent and collapsed face-first on his cot. Some witnesses said he burst into tears. Others said he just took a nap. Either way, by the time he came back outside, he had made a major decision.

Grant ordered his army to pack up and prepare to move. *Here we go again,* thought discouraged Union soldiers. Every year so far they had marched into Virginia, fought Lee's army, lost, and retreated back to the North.

But as this march began, the men noticed that they weren't heading north. They were marching farther south. They were continuing their drive toward Richmond.

"Our spirits rose," said a Union soldier. "The men began to sing."

A newspaper reporter asked Grant if he had any message for Abraham Lincoln. Yes, Grant said: "If you see the president, tell him, from me, that whatever happens there will be no turning back."

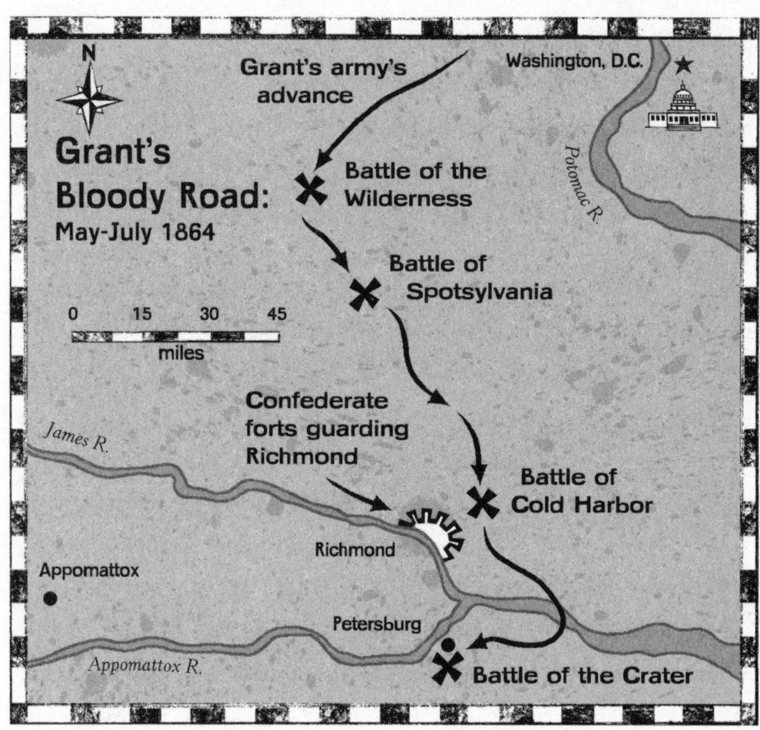

Spotsylvania Horrors

Robert E. Lee was not surprised. "General Grant will not retreat," Lee predicted after the battle of the Wilderness. "He will move to Spotsylvania."

Lee rushed his soldiers south to Spotsylvania—and got there just in time to prepare for another massive attack by Grant's army. At first Union soldiers started gaining ground. Lee rode to the front of his army and prepared to lead a charge himself.

But his men refused to budge. Southern soldiers would do anything for General Lee—except allow him to get shot.

"General Lee to the rear!" someone shouted.

Then all the soldiers, young men who had never given an order in their lives, were suddenly bossing around their commander. "General Lee to the rear!" they yelled. "General Lee to the rear!"

Lee replied: "If you will promise me to drive those people from our works, I will go back!"

The men cheered in agreement. Then they charged forward, and drove "those people" back.

The battle of Spotsylvania raged on day after day, and soldiers who had seen years of combat said it was the most terrifying battle yet. The two armies blasted and stabbed at each other from just a few feet away, while rain poured down and wounded men slowly sank into the bloody mud. "I never expect to be fully believed when I tell what I saw of the horrors at Spotsylvania," said a Union officer.

After a week of these horrors, Grant called off the attack. Once again, he had lost far more men than Lee. And once again, he packed up and moved his army south. One more big attack, Grant thought, and he could smash his way through to Richmond. "Lee's army is really whipped," Grant said.

He had never been more wrong in his life.

June 3: I Was Killed

While walking through camp on the night of June 2, a Union officer noticed something very strange:

> *"The men were calmly writing their names and home addresses on slips of paper and pinning them on the backs of their coats, so that their bodies might be recognized and their fate made known to their families at home."* 
>
> ***Horace Porter***

Grant's men were camped at a place called Cold Harbor. Their orders were to attack Lee's army before sunrise. Grant was confident this attack would succeed—but his soldiers seemed to know better. They knew Lee was out there, ready and waiting for them.

One young soldier actually skipped ahead one day in his diary and wrote: "June 3, 1864. Cold Harbor. I was killed."

The Union attack began at four-thirty the next morning. "We started with a yell," said a Massachusetts soldier named Harvey Clark.

"To your guns, boys—they're charging!" shouted Southern soldiers.

Harvey Clark was one of about 60,000 Union men charging right toward those guns—and the entire army slammed face-first into what Clark described as a "solid sheet of fire."

"It seemed more like a volcanic blast than a battle," said another Union soldier.

Nearly 8,000 Union soldiers were shot, most of them in the first ten minutes of fighting. "The dead covered five acres of ground about as thickly as they could be laid," a Confederate officer later said. Among the dead was the soldier who had predicted his own death in his diary the night before.

"I regret this assault more than any one I have ever ordered," Grant told his officers that night.

He was even more depressed when he read what Northern newspapers were saying about him now. "They call me a butcher," Grant grumbled.

The Ticking Clock

So let's review: Grant's plan was a miserable, bloody disaster. Except for one small detail: it was working.

Even after the slaughter at Cold Harbor, Grant continued fighting his way south. New soldiers arrived from the North, so Grant's army was still twice as large as Lee's. And by the end of June, Grant had Lee's army nearly surrounded in the town of Petersburg, just twenty-five miles from Richmond.

Meanwhile, down in Georgia, General William T. Sherman pushed Confederate forces all the way to the edge of Atlanta. Home to weapons factories and key railroad lines, Atlanta was a city the South simply could not afford to lose.

Now it was all a question of timing. As the summer sped past, Sherman tried to fight his way into Atlanta. And Grant was still stuck outside of Petersburg. The Union needed a big victory, and the clock was ticking.

Not that Southern soldiers were enjoying the summer. In Petersburg, Lee's soldiers were living in filthy trenches, in constant danger from Union bullets and bombs. Food shortages got so bad that the men were regularly given bags of rotting corn filled with squirming worms. One soldier remembered the men getting hunks of bacon that were "scaly" and "spotted" and gave off "a stinking smell when boiled. You could put a piece in your mouth and chew it for a long time, and the longer you chewed it the bigger it got. Then, by desperate effort, you would gulp it down."

The South was running out of food. But the North was running out of time.

Waiting for News

Lincoln was so anxious for some good news, he was hardly able to sleep at night, and he walked around the White House with black bags under his eyes. An artist who was painting a picture of Lincoln at this time said of the president's face: "There were days when I could scarcely look into it without crying."

There was some news in July, but it wasn't too good. A small Southern force had fought its way inside the borders of Washington, D.C., and was now just a few miles from the White House. Lincoln went out to have a look at the fighting. He stood on the wall of a fort as bullets zoomed past. Standing six foot four, with a tall black hat, he was the most obvious target in the city.

"Mr. President, you are standing within range of five hundred rebel rifles," cautioned a Union soldier.

Another soldier was more direct: "Get down, you damn fool, before you get shot!"

Lincoln got down.

The Southern soldiers were chased from the capital, but soon there was more bad news—this time from Grant.

This story begins in Petersburg, Virginia, where the enemy armies were living in trenches just 150 yards apart. In one of the Union trenches, a few Pennsylvania soldiers looked out at the Confederate fort protecting Petersburg. These guys were coal miners—experts at digging tunnels. And now one of them had an idea:

"We could blow that fort out of existence if we could run a mine shaft under it."

The Pennsylvania boys got permission to give it a try. And in just four weeks they pulled off one of the great engineering feats of the war—a 511-foot tunnel that ended twenty feet below the Confederate fort. They opened up a huge room at the end of the tunnel and filled it with 320 barrels of gunpowder. Then they attached a long fuse to the gunpowder.

The fuse was lit at 3:15 a.m. on July 30. Thousands of Union soldiers crouched nearby, ready to attack right after the explosion. The fuse should have reached the gunpowder in fifteen minutes. But fifteen minutes passed, then thirty, then forty-five...

A soldier named Harry Reese volunteered to enter the tunnel and find out what had gone wrong. He saw that the fuse had burned out. He relit it—and ran for his life.

Moments after Reese dove out of the tunnel opening, soldiers heard a low rumble that sounded like distant thunder. "Suddenly the earth trembled beneath our feet," a Union soldier remembered. Then red flames shot up from cracks in the ground, and a massive section of earth lifted up into the air and seemed to float there like an island in the sky.

The blast woke up thousands of Confederate soldiers—many of them were in the air at the time. One man remembered opening his eyes while flying through the air and seeing his own arms and legs swinging wildly. He passed out, landed hard, and lived.

But more than 250 Confederate soldiers were killed in the blast, and thousands more panicked and ran. This was the opportunity of a lifetime for the Union army. But the Northern soldiers just stood there. They were just as shocked as the Southerners by the gigantic explosion and the huge crater that now lay at their feet. Even worse, the Union general who was supposed to lead the attack got scared and hid in a ditch and started guzzling rum. By the time the Union soldiers finally attacked, they were too late and too disorganized. Another 4,000 Union men were killed or wounded—and the Union army accomplished nothing.

Grant called the Battle of the Crater "the saddest affair I have witnessed in the war."

Lincoln was not too pleased about it, either.

"Deader Than Dead"

Many Northerners were now convinced that they could not win this war. And they were furious with Lincoln for continuing to send young men to fight and die. A woman named Sarah Butler summed up this anger:

> *"What is all this struggling and fighting for? This ruin and death to thousands of families?"*
>
> ***Sarah Butler***

Former presidents spoke out against Lincoln. Newspapers called for him to drop out of the presidential race. A Democratic Party newspaper reported with glee: "Lincoln is deader than dead." Even Republican leaders turned against him. "I told Mr. Lincoln that his re-election was an impossibility," a top Republican said. "The people are wild for peace."

What could be worse for Abe Lincoln? How about this: it looked as if he was going to lose his job to none other than George McClellan. That's right, the former Union general who had once referred to Lincoln as "the original gorilla." McClellan was chosen to be the Democratic candidate for president in 1864. He promised to bring a quick end to the war.

"I am going to be beaten," Lincoln said in August. "And unless some great change takes place, badly beaten."

Some Great Change Takes Place

William T. Sherman could not sit still—or shut up. "The most restless man in the army" was how one officer described Sherman. Men who served with him said it was always exciting when he entered the room, and always a great relief when he left.

For a man who never stopped talking, Sherman needed only a few words to announce the biggest news of the war so far. On September 3, 1864, he sent a telegram to Washington saying: "Atlanta is ours, and fairly won."

Yes, after months of marching and fighting in Georgia, Sherman's army had just captured the key city of Atlanta. With the elections coming up, this changed everything. Suddenly it looked as if the Union actually could win the war.

"Since Atlanta I have felt as if all were dead within me," said Mary Chesnut of South Carolina. "We are going to be wiped off the earth."

Election Day, 1864

November 8, Election Day, was cool and rainy in Washington, D.C. After work, Abraham Lincoln walked from the White House to the telegraph office in the War Department building. While waiting for news from around the country, Lincoln served plates of fried oysters to his cabinet members. And he kept everyone calm by telling funny stories that began with lines such as, "You know, that reminds me of a feller I knew in Illinois . . ."

Then the election returns started coming in, and the news was good:

	Abraham Lincoln *(Republican)*	**George McClellan** *Democrat)*
Electoral Votes:	212	21
Popular Votes:	2,213,665	1,805,237
Percentage of total vote:	55%	45%
Percentage of soldiers' vote:	78%	22%

Lincoln's strong support from Union soldiers turned out to be a key to his victory. Winning seventy-eight percent of this vote is amazing when you think that soldiers were basically voting on whether or not to continue the war. They wanted peace more than anyone—but they also wanted to finish the job they had begun. As one Union soldier put it: "I had rather stay out here a lifetime, much as I dislike it, than consent to a division of our country."

When the election results reached Grant's army at Petersburg, the men broke out in loud cheers. Lee's men heard the noise and called across the open space between enemy trenches:

Southern Soldier: *Say, Yank!*

Northern Soldier: *Hello, Johnny!*

Southern Soldier: *Don't fire, Yank.*

Northern Soldier: *All right, Johnny.*

Southern Soldier: *What are y'all cheering for?*

Northern Soldier: *Big victory on our side.*

Southern Soldier: *What is it, Yank?*

Northern Soldier: *Old Abe has cleaned all your fellers out up North.*

Lincoln's election was a crushing disappointment to the South. But Jefferson Davis was still committed to victory. "We will be free," he vowed. "We will govern ourselves . . . if we have to see every Southern plantation sacked, and every Southern city in flames."

Speaking of plantations and cities in flames . . .

Why the South Hates Sherman

A few weeks after the election, Dolly Lunt looked out the window of her plantation home in Georgia and saw a large group of Union soldiers marching toward her yard. As soon as they got there, the soldiers started stealing everything in sight.

"Like demons they rush in!" she wrote to a friend, "Breaking locks and whatever is in their way. The thousand pounds of meat in my smoke-house is gone in a twinkling, my flour, my meat, my lard, butter, eggs, pickles of various kinds . . . wine, jars, and jugs are all gone. My eighteen fat turkeys, my hens, chickens, and fowls, my young pigs, are shot down in my yard and hunted as if they were rebels themselves."

She ran outside and found a Union officer and begged him for help.

He shrugged and said, "I cannot help you, madam, it is orders."

Lunt watched helplessly as the soldiers rode off with her horses, mules, and sheep. And of course, slaves living on the plantation took the opportunity to escape.

This was all part of Sherman's plan to end the war. After capturing Atlanta (and burning much of it to the ground) Sherman divided his army in two. He sent half of it, under General George Thomas, to chase after the Confederate army that had been defeated at Atlanta. Sherman personally led the other half on a march through Georgia, destroying farms, burning buildings, ripping up railroads. Sherman wanted to make it painfully clear to white Southern families that the Confederate army was no longer strong enough to protect them. He wanted to convince Southerners that it was foolish to continue supporting this war. "I can make the march," he told Grant, "and make Georgia howl!"

Sherman knew this was a cruel way to fight, but he saw it as the best way to end the war:

"War is cruelty. There is no use trying to reform it. The crueler it is, the sooner it will be over."

William T. Sherman

With this idea in mind, Sherman led his army of 60,000 on a 285-mile march from Atlanta all the way to the Atlantic Ocean. For Union soldiers, this was like a vacation. With plenty to eat and no fighting to do, the men sang as they marched. One favorite song began: "We will hang Jeff Davis on a sour apple tree."

The people in Sherman's path, meanwhile, shook with rage. Eliza Andrews was shocked to see the blackened remains of buildings, and farm animals killed and left on the ground to rot. "The stench in some places was unbearable," she said. "I almost felt as if I should like to hang a Yankee myself."

Sherman's army reached the sea in late December. He sent a quick telegram to President Lincoln, saying: "I beg to present you, as a Christmas gift, the city of Savannah."

Then he marched his army into South Carolina, the state where the Civil War began. "We will let her know that it isn't so sweet to secede as she thought it would be," said one Union soldier. And Sherman's soldiers continued slicing a wide wound through the South.

Now you know why, to this day, one of the most hated men in the southern United States is William Tecumseh Sherman.

Lincoln Looks Ahead

The war was not over yet. But in Washington, D.C., Abraham Lincoln and members of Congress were already making plans for Reconstruction—the long process of putting the country back together again. In January 1865, for example, Congress approved the Thirteenth Amendment to the Constitution. This amendment forever banned slavery everywhere in the United States.

"I have felt, ever since the vote, as if I were in a new country," said George Julian, a member of Congress from Indiana.

At his inauguration ceremony in March, Lincoln also looked to the future. As he often did so well, he put very big ideas into just a few words:

> *"With malice toward none, with charity for all, with firmness in the right as God gives us to see the right, let us strive on to finish the work we are in, to bind up the nation's wounds, to care for him who shall have borne the battle and for his widow and his orphan, to do all which may achieve and cherish a just and lasting peace among ourselves and with all nations. "*

Frederick Douglass was impressed by Lincoln's words. Douglass, who had grown up in slavery, had seen amazing changes in his life. And now he did something that would have been unthinkable just a few years before. There would be a party that night at the White House to celebrate Lincoln's inauguration. No African American had ever been invited to the president's home. Douglass decided to go.

Things did not go smoothly.

"On reaching the door," Douglass later said, "two policemen stationed there took me rudely by the arm and ordered me to stand back, for their directions were to admit no persons of my color."

Douglass knew this order did not come from Lincoln. "I shall not go out of this building till I see President Lincoln," he told the guards.

The argument continued until someone finally recognized Douglass and told the police to let him in. Douglass saw Lincoln standing inside, towering over a crowd of supporters.

"Here comes my friend Douglass," Lincoln announced.

The men shook hands and had this conversation:

Lincoln: *I'm glad to see you. I saw you in the crowd today, listening to my inaugural address; how did you like it?*
Douglass: *Mr. Lincoln, I must not detain you with my poor opinion, when there are thousands waiting to shake hands with you.*
Lincoln: *No, no, you must stop a little, Douglass; there is no man in the country whose opinion I value more than yours. I want to know what you think of it?*
Douglass: *Mr. Lincoln, that was a sacred effort.*
Lincoln: *I'm glad you liked it!*

Lincoln and Douglass were looking forward to a better future. But the process of Reconstruction couldn't really begin yet, for one simple reason. The South was still determined to win this war.

Empty Stomachs and Brave Hearts

That was going to be a problem.

After suffering through winter in their trenches in Petersburg, Lee's army was growing weaker and weaker. The South was so short on metal to make weapons, soldiers were given rewards for chasing after Union bombs and bringing in pieces of them. The metal was then recycled into new weapons. But food remained the real problem. After months of hunger, soldiers simply could not continue to do their jobs. Their bodies began to break down, and they became dizzy and exhausted after just a few minutes of work.

To make things worse, many of Lee's men were getting desperate letters from home. Families were running out of food too, and they begged their husbands and sons to come home and help. One soldier got a letter from his wife that began: "Edward, unless you come home we must die."

Could you resist a letter like that? Thousands of men couldn't, and in the early months of 1865, Lee's army began to melt away.

On April 1, Lee decided his army was no longer strong enough to continue protecting Richmond. Lee had one last hope—march west and try to join up with what was left of Joseph Johnston's army. Together, the armies might have enough men to continue fighting.

Lee's men moved "with empty stomachs and brave hearts," remembered Carlton McCarthy. Some soldiers actually slept as they walked. All that was left for food was dried-out corn meant for the horses. The men roasted the stuff and chewed it till their gums bled. They stumbled on, all the while being chased and bombed by Grant's army.

Waking from the Nightmare

Back in Richmond, Agnes Pryor was sitting in church on April 2. She saw a messenger tiptoe up to Jefferson Davis. "A note was handed to President Davis." she said. "He rose instantly, and walked down the aisle—his face set, so we could read nothing."

Something was very wrong. And the news soon spread: Lee's army was heading west. Richmond was wide open to Grant's army.

Davis and the rest of the Confederate government packed up and rushed out of town. But first they destroyed everything they couldn't carry—their remaining supplies of weapons and the Confederate ships in the harbor.

Before sunrise on April 3, Union soldiers near Richmond woke to the sounds of those weapons and ships blowing up. "We were startled by heavy explosions," remembered an African American soldier named John C. Brock. "There was also a great light seen in the direction of Richmond, which led us to suppose there was something more than usual going on."

A few hours later, Brock was among thousands of Union soldiers marching into a city out of control. "Richmond was literally a sea of flame," one soldier said. Bombs were bursting in warehouses, sparks were shooting from ships on the river, bells were clanging, people were jumping out of burning buildings, and thieves were breaking out of jail and running around looting stores and homes. But the most amazing part of the scene was that black soldiers were among the first Union troops to march into the Confederate capital. Men and women who had been slaves the day before lined the streets, shouting and cheering and crying. John C. Brock described the scene: "Old men and women, tottering on their canes, would make their way to a Union soldier, catch him by the hand, and exclaim, 'Thank God, honey, that I have lived to see this day!'"

Lincoln felt the same. "Thank God I have lived to see this," he said when he heard that Richmond had finally been captured. "It seems to me that I have been dreaming a horrid dream for four years, and now the nightmare is gone." Then, as if to make sure the dream really was over, he said, "I want to see Richmond."

Lincoln showed up the next day—though the ship of marines that was supposed to guard him got lost on the river. With only a few sailors for guards, he walked through the streets of Richmond. Freed African Americans cheered and sang, while white residents watched Lincoln from the windows of their homes. Lincoln continued two miles to the Confederate White House, went inside, and sat down in Jefferson Davis's chair. Happy and exhausted, he turned to one of the sailors and said: "I wonder if I could get a glass of water?"

Meeting at Appomattox

On April 9, Lee's small army reached the small town of Appomattox Court House. Grant soon had him surrounded. Lee had no choice now but to surrender. He put on a fancy new uniform and said: "There is nothing left for me to do but to go and see General Grant, and I would rather die a thousand deaths."

The enemy generals agreed to meet at a nearby house. But unlike Lee, Grant didn't think to change into a clean uniform. As he walked into the house, Grant noticed that his clothes were dusty and wrinkled. It was a little embarrassing. "In my rough traveling suit," he said, "I must have contrasted very strangely with a man so handsomely dressed, six feet high and of faultless form."

The whole meeting was fairly awkward. Lee and Grant began by chatting about the fine weather, and about the Mexican War, in which both men had served long ago. Grant was too polite to bring up the reason they were there, so he just kept making small talk. Lee finally had to break in.

"I have come to meet you," Lee said, "about the surrender of my army."

Then they got down to business—and quickly agreed on an official surrender.

As the news sped though Grant's camp, soldiers erupted in cheers and started throwing hats, boots, knapsacks, and everything else into the air. One soldier remembered the scene:

"They fall on each other's necks and laugh and cry by turns. Huge, lumbering, bearded men embrace and kiss like schoolgirls, then dance and sing and shout, stand on their heads and play leapfrog with each other."

Stephen Minot Weld

Union gunners began firing cannons in celebration, but Grant ordered the noisy party to stop. "The war is over," he told his army. "The rebels are our countrymen again."

Everyone was silent at the surrender ceremony as Lee's men marched out to stack up their guns. Tears ran down the cheeks of Southern soldiers as they laid down the bullet-torn flags they had carried into so many deadly fights. Men on both sides seemed to be in shock—they had begun to believe they would be fighting forever.

Joshua Chamberlain (who had led Union troops to victory on Little Round Top at Gettysburg) was thinking the same thing men on both sides were thinking: "It is by miracles that we have lived to see this day—any of us standing here."

600,000 Plus One

The remaining Southern armies surrendered over the next few weeks, bringing the war to an end. More than 600,000 soldiers died in the Civil War, making it by far the deadliest conflict in American history. And when you count up the Civil War dead, you really have to include Abraham Lincoln.

On April 11, Lincoln stood on the balcony of the White House and spoke to a small crowd about his plans for Reconstruction. In the crowd was a twenty-six-year-old actor from Virginia named John Wilkes Booth. "That is the last speech he will ever make," Booth muttered.

Plenty of Southerners hated Lincoln, but Booth took it to an extreme. A few months before, he had quit his successful acting career to focus full-time on trying to kidnap the president. His first plan was to grab Lincoln from a balcony in a theater, tie him to his chair, and lower him with ropes to the ground. But this was just too complicated. Booth decided it would be simpler to shoot Lincoln.

On April 14, newspapers announced that Abraham and Mary Lincoln, along with their guests Ulysses and Julia Grant, would be attending the play *Our American Cousin* at Ford's Theatre that night. Booth decided this was his chance.

Lincoln was in a good mood that day. He took a carriage ride with Mary, and they looked forward to better days ahead. "We must both be more cheerful in the future," he said. "Between the war and the loss of our darling Willie, we have been very miserable."

Lincoln was disappointed when Grant announced that he and his wife were going to skip the play. They wanted to go visit their children in New Jersey, Grant explained, and their train was leaving in a few hours. Lincoln decided he didn't want to go to the play either. But the papers had announced he would be there, and he didn't want to disappoint people by not showing up.

By the time the Lincolns got to the theater, the play had already started. The actors stopped acting, though, and everyone cheered the president and his wife as they settled into their seats. Then the play continued.

John Wilkes Booth knew this theater well from his acting days. At about ten p.m. he walked up to the balcony and silently opened the door of Lincoln's private box. A policeman was supposed to be guarding the box—but he found the play boring, so he went across the street to get a drink. Booth was able to walk right in, pull out a small pistol, and shoot Lincoln in the back of the head.

Then Booth leaped down from the balcony, breaking his left leg as he slammed into the stage below. The entire audience watched in shock as Booth limped out the side door. He got on his horse and rode away.

A doctor named Charles Leale rushed to Lincoln's box and inspected Lincoln's wound. Leale was only twenty-three, but he had experience as an army surgeon—he knew bullet wounds. "I can't save him," Leale said. "It is impossible for him to recover."

Lincoln died at 7:22 the next morning.

"Now he belongs to the ages," said the secretary of war, Edwin Stanton.

Stuck with Each Other

Abraham Lincoln had saved the Union and ended slavery—not a bad four years' work. But now he was gone, and the United States faced a Reconstruction process full of questions and challenges. Whatever the future would bring, one thing was clear: all Americans were in it together now.

This idea was beautifully summed up by Ely Parker, a Union officer (and Seneca Indian) who worked on General Grant's staff. Back at that meeting at Appomattox—the one where Lee surrendered his army to Grant—Grant introduced Lee to the members of his staff. As Lee shook Parker's hand, he noticed that Parker was a Native American.

"I am glad to see one real American here," Lee said.

Parker replied, "We are all Americans."

What Ever Happened to . . . ?

Nicknamed "the Angel of the Battlefield," **Clara Barton** continued nursing wounded soldiers throughout the war. Then she went on to found the American Red Cross, an organization dedicated to providing aid to victims of wars and natural disasters. And she didn't just sit in her office. When the Spanish-American War broke out in 1898, the seventy-seven-year-old Barton brought medical supplies to American soldiers on the battlefield in Cuba. Two years later, when a hurricane devastated Galveston, Texas, Barton rushed to the scene to distribute food and medicine. She retired in 1904, at the age of eighty-three.

Killing President Lincoln was just part of **John Wilkes Booth**'s larger plan to destroy the U.S. government, and, in his twisted mind, avenge his beloved Confederacy. While Booth was shooting Lincoln, Booth's friend Lewis Powell charged into the home of the secretary of state, William Seward, and stabbed him in the face and neck. Seward recovered; Powell was captured and hanged. A third member of Booth's gang was supposed to murder Vice President Andrew Johnson. But he chickened out and got drunk instead. He was hanged too.

Booth, meanwhile, escaped from Ford's Theatre on horseback and raced to the home of his friend Dr. Samuel Mudd, who treated his broken leg. Over the next two weeks, Union soldiers chased Booth through Maryland and into Virginia, where they finally trapped him in a barn. When Booth refused to come out, soldiers set the barn on fire and shot into the burning building. A bullet sliced open Booth's neck, and he died muttering, "Useless, useless . . ."

After serving time in a Northern prison for spying, **Belle Boyd** sailed for Britain in 1864. And when her ship was captured by the Union navy, her story took another amazing turn—she and the Union sailor in charge of guarding her fell in love. Boyd convinced him to run away with her, and their marriage, in London, was headline news across Europe and in America. Boyd began an acting career in Britain, returned to the United States after the war, and continued performing on stage until her death in 1900.

Defending his beating of Senator Charles Sumner, **Preston Brooks** insisted that he had gone easy on Sumner. "If I desired to kill the Senator, why did not I do it?" Brooks asked. "You all admit that I had him in my power." Facing possible punishment from Congress, Brooks resigned from the House—but was immediately reelected by South Carolina voters. He triumphantly returned to Washington and served until his death in 1857. He was thirty-eight years old.

John Burns recovered from the wounds he got at the battle of Gettysburg. Soon newspaper reporters and photographers started showing up at his house, eager to tell the story of the seventy-year-old soldier. When Abraham Lincoln came to town to give the Gettysburg Address, he met the famous Burns, and the two men chatted as they walked down the street. Burns refused to make a big deal of his role in the battle, though. When asked about it, he simply said, "Oh, I pitched in with them Wisconsin fellers."

Still recovering from his Fort Wagner battle wounds, **William Carney** moved back to Massachusetts, found work as a mail carrier, and married a woman named Susannah. He was the first African American to be awarded the Congressional Medal of Honor, but it took a while—he didn't actually get the award until 1900. When he died eight years later, flags across Massachusetts were lowered to half-mast, the first time this honor had been given to an African American citizen.

The young drummer boy **Johnny Clem** served with the Union army through the end of the war. Then Ulysses S. Grant tried to help get Clem into the U.S. Military Academy at West Point, but Clem kept failing the entrance exam. So Clem returned to the army and stayed there his entire career, gradually rising to the rank of general. When he finally decided to retire in 1915, he was the only Civil War veteran still left in the army.

Jefferson Davis did not agree that the South had lost the Civil War. Determined to carry on the fight for Southern independence, Davis was hoping to slip into the mountains of the South and continue leading the war from there. A month after Lee's surrender, however, Davis was surrounded and grabbed by Union soldiers in Georgia. A rumor soon spread that he had been trying to escape disguised as a woman: "Jeff Davis Captured in Hoop Skirts" announced one Northern newspaper. But this wasn't quite accurate. What probably happened was that as Union soldiers closed in, Jefferson's wife, Varina, threw her shawl over her husband, hoping to hide his famous head. So he was captured wearing her shawl, not her dress.

Davis spent the next two years in prison, charged with treason against the United States. He was never actually put on trial, though, and was released in 1867. Right up until his death in 1889, Davis continued to proudly insist that the South had been justified in seceding from the Union.

After her husband's death, **Varina Davis** shocked her Southern friends by moving to New York City and supporting herself by writing newspaper articles. One day there was a knock on Varina's hotel room door. She opened the door and the woman in the doorway said:

"Hello, I am Mrs. Grant."

"I am very glad to meet you," Varina said to Julia Grant. "Come in."

Varina Davis and Julia Grant became close friends and were often seen around town together. Both women hoped their visible friendship would help heal the deep wounds left by the Civil War. Varina lived well into the twentieth century—she even rode in a car in 1906 (she didn't like it). She died in New York, but was buried beside her husband in Richmond.

After the war **Frederick Douglass** continued his nonstop travels, speaking and writing in defense of the rights of African Americans. While traveling in Maryland in 1877, Douglass was surprised to get a note from Thomas Auld, the man who had owned him nearly forty years before.

Auld was dying and wanted to see Douglass one last time. Douglass entered the house and stepped up to Auld's bedside. Auld reached out a trembling hand, and Douglass took it in his own. Then Auld began to weep. Douglass sat down and the two men talked over old times. Then Douglass got back to work. "Forty years of my life have been given to the cause of my people," he wrote in his autobiography. "And if I had forty years more they should all be sacredly given to the great cause."

After losing the presidential election of 1860 to Abraham Lincoln, **Stephen "the Little Giant" Douglas** truly acted like a giant. Putting aside his bitter rivalry with Lincoln, Douglas promised to do everything in his power to help the new president save the Union. As the two men shook hands, tears came to Lincoln's eyes and he said, "God bless you, Douglas." Douglas used every ounce of energy in his body trying to persuade Southerners to give President Lincoln a chance. Weakened, exhausted, and disappointed, he died of a fever in June 1861, two months after the war began.

Sarah Emma Edmonds, or "Frank Thompson" as she was known to her fellow Union soldiers, served in the Union army as a nurse and spy—and her secret identity was never discovered. She volunteered for several dangerous spying missions, sneaking behind enemy lines disguised as characters including an escaped slave and an overweight Irish peddler named "Bridget O'Shea." Edmonds married after the war and had three sons. "I am naturally fond of adventure," she said. "But patriotism was the true secret of my success."

Ulysses S. Grant always regretted not going to the play with Lincoln that famous night. Had he been there, he wondered, would he have heard Booth opening the door to Lincoln's box? Could he have grabbed Booth before the killer had a chance to pull the trigger?

Just forty-three years old when the war ended, Grant decided to start a new career in politics. And he got off to a good start, winning the presidential election of 1868. But it turned out he was a much better soldier than politician. He had the embarrassing habit of giving key government jobs to old army friends who were completely unqualified.

After two terms in the White House, Ulysses and Julia Grant moved to New York City, where Ulysses immediately lost all their money in bad investments. Then his doctor told him he had throat cancer and had only a few months to live. Displaying his famously fierce determination, Grant raced against death to finish an autobiography, which he hoped would earn some money for his family. Wrapped in blankets, suffering from soaring fevers and piercing pain, Grant finished the book just days before he died. *The Personal Memoirs of U.S. Grant* was a huge success. Later that year the publishers handed Julia Grant a check for $200,000.

"Wild Rose" O'Neal Greenhow spied for the Confederacy until Union police kicked her out of Washington, D.C., in 1862. Next, at Jefferson Davis's request, she traveled to Europe and tried to persuade big shots there to support the South. Sailing back to the Confederacy in 1864, her ship was chased by a Union gunboat and slammed into a sandbar off the coast of North Carolina. Determined to avoid capture, Greenhow jumped onto a lifeboat and rowed toward land. The boat tipped over in a storm and she drowned.

Exhausted and broke after the war, **Robert E. Lee** took the job of president of Washington College in Virginia (now Washington and Lee University). Lee needed the income, but he also wanted to set an example for his fellow Southerners; he urged them to put the war behind them and help prepare the country for a better future. "We wish now for good feeling to grow up between North and South," he said.

Lee's health never fully recovered from four years of war, and his body weakened quickly in the fall of 1870. One afternoon as Lee was leaving his office, a student showed up with Lee's picture, hoping the general would sign it for a girl he knew back home. But Lee looked very tired, so the student said he'd come back some other time. "No," Lee said, "I will go right back and do it now." It was the last time Lee signed his name. He died at home two weeks later.

"There was a cheerless cold rain and everything seemed gloomy." That's how the secretary of the navy, Gideon Welles, described the morning of April 15, the morning **Abraham Lincoln** died. Welles watched Lincoln breathe his last breath, then walked to the White House, where he saw hundreds of African American women and children standing in front of the building, crying in the rain.

The shocking news of Lincoln's death spread across the nation that morning.

People in Philadelphia read the news on their way to work, and the city's streetcars were soon filled with weeping men. In Boston a thousand people started marching together through the street—not knowing why, just silently marching. Church bells tolled all over the North, and colorful flags celebrating the Union victory were taken down. Teachers told their students to go home, there would be no school that day.

White Southerners were stunned too, for a different reason. Mary Chesnut spoke for many when she said, "I know this foul murder will bring upon us worse miseries." She may not have liked Lincoln, but she feared that without his strong leadership and sense of justice, the process of Reconstruction was going to be much harder on the South. She was right.

Lincoln's body, meanwhile, was taken by train from Washington to Springfield, Illinois—the same route Lincoln had taken from Springfield to Washington just over four years before. After facing fierce criticism every day of his presidency, Lincoln would probably be amazed to find out that these days historians usually rank him as the greatest president in American history.

Life never got any easier for **Mary Lincoln**. Never really recovered from the death of her son Willie, she was shattered by the shock of seeing her husband murdered. After selling her jewelry and clothes to pay off family debts, Mary sailed to Europe with her son Tad. Just as they were becoming best friends, she watched him get sick and die at the age of eighteen. "Now in this world," she said, "there is nothing left for me but the deepest anguish and desolation." Mary began showing signs of mental illness, often sitting alone in the dark and mumbling about people who were trying to kill her. Her only remaining son, Robert, actually had her declared insane. After being confined in a nursing home for a few months, Mary moved into her sister's house in Springfield, Illinois. She died there in 1882 and was buried beside her husband.

James Longstreet, the man General Lee called "My Old War Horse," fought by Lee's side until the surrender at Appomattox. But people always need someone to blame when they lose a war, and Southerners loved Lee too much to pick him. So they blamed Longstreet, claiming he had failed to follow Lee's orders at key battles such as Gettysburg. Longstreet defended himself, suggesting that Lee's poor strategy at Gettysburg had been the real cause of defeat. For this he was considered a traitor by many Southerners. Luckily, tempers have calmed a bit over 150 years, and Longstreet's reputation as a soldier has been making a strong comeback.

George McClellan thought voters had made a poor choice in selecting Lincoln over him in the presidential election of 1864. Still, he was a bit relieved he would not have to run the country. "I feel that a great weight is removed from my mind," he said. McClellan began writing a book about his experiences in the war, hoping, as he said, "to place my side of the story on the record." His book was destroyed in a fire, though, and before he could finish rewriting it, he died unexpectedly at the age of fifty-eight. One of Mac's friends finished the book for him, calling it *McClellan's Own Story* and spicing it up by adding the general's private letters—letters with nasty remarks about Abraham Lincoln that poor Mac had never intended to be made public. Said one harsh reviewer of *McClellan's Own Story:* "It were better for his memory had he left his story untold."

The Union soldier **John Ransom** survived fourteen months as a prisoner of war, watching many friends die of starvation and disease. He escaped, was captured, escaped again, and finally made it to freedom thanks to several enslaved men and women who fed him and guided him to a Union army camp. He was thrilled to see soldiers from his hometown, and he recalled they "could hardly believe it was myself that appeared to them." With good reason—the Union army had reported Ransom dead a year before. But he was very much alive, and stayed that way until 1919.

"I am sick and tired of fighting," **William T. Sherman** griped at the end of the war. But he was a soldier at heart, and he stayed in the army, taking over from Grant as top commander in 1869. This was a time when the army was battling several Native American tribes in the West. Sherman drove the tribes onto reservations using the same merciless fighting style he had used in the South. He retired in 1884 and spent the last few years of his life doing what he really loved: going to the theater and attending fancy dinner parties at least four nights a week. Wherever he went he was surrounded by former soldiers who wanted to shake his hand. They called him "Uncle Billy." He called them "my boys."

Just how important was **Harriet Beecher Stowe**'s book *Uncle Tom's Cabin?* When Stowe visited the White House during the war, Abraham Lincoln supposedly said to her: "So you're the little woman who wrote the book that started this Great War!" Stowe's long writing career included thirty much less famous books, none of which caused armed conflict. She and her family moved around a bit, finally settling in Hartford, Connecticut, where she lived next door to Mark Twain.

Suffering from headaches and nightmares, **Charles Sumner** did not return to the Senate until 1859, three years after being beaten by Preston Brooks. He resumed his role as a leading abolitionist, and after the war he tried to persuade Congress to pass a bill banning racial segregation in the United States. On his deathbed in 1874, surrounded by senators, his final words were: "Save my civil rights bill." And Congress did pass a civil rights law banning segregation—ninety years later.

After cruising the Confederate ship *Planter* to freedom, **Robert Smalls** continued working as a naval pilot—only now he was a free man, fighting for the Union. He returned to South Carolina after the war and bought the house in which he and his family had lived as slaves. Elected to the U.S. House of Representatives in 1874, Smalls spoke out often against new laws in the South that were denying African Americans the rights they had won after the Civil War. "All they need," Smalls said of his fellow African Americans, "is an equal chance in the battle of life."

On her way back to New York after war, **Harriet Tubman** got a cruel preview of the rough road ahead for African Americans in both the North and South. As her train passed through New Jersey, a conductor told her that black passengers were not welcome in the main car. "Hustle out of here," he said, telling her to go sit with the baggage. She refused. He tried to grab her, but she was too strong for him. Finally three men lifted Tubman and tossed her into the baggage car, breaking her arm in the process.

Tubman lived another forty-eight years, and she was busy the entire time. In addition to speaking at women's voting rights meetings, she was dedicated to helping African Americans in her community. In 1908 she opened Harriet Tubman House, a home for poor and elderly African Americans. She was eighty-five.

Under the name "Lieutenant Harry T. Buford," **Loreta Janeta Velazquez** fought in several major battles and was wounded at Shiloh while burying bodies near the battlefield. When the surgeon treating her discovered her secret, Velazquez quit the army and decided to become a spy instead. Now wearing women's clothing, she somehow managed to sit in on strategy meetings with Abraham Lincoln. At least, that's what she said in her 1876 autobiography, *The Woman in Battle.* To this day, historians disagree about how much of her book is true.

Source Notes

Here's a typical day for me: I spend ten hours in the library reading tall stacks of books and taking tons of notes. Yes, I basically do homework for a living. But I like it, actually. I find stories and characters that interest me and I follow them around, jumping from one book to another, chasing down leads in a search for ever-better details and quotes. I sometimes think of myself as a kind of detective—a story detective.

The point is, I ended up reading hundreds of books while writing *Two Miserable Presidents*. Below is a list of the ones I found most useful. If you want to learn more about the people and events of the Civil War, this list would be a good place to start. I hope it's helpful.

Books about the Civil War

I started my research by reading a bunch of books about the Civil War—books that cover the entire war. When you read books like this you don't get too much detail about any one person or event, but you get a great overall picture of what happened and why.

Catton, Bruce. *The Centennial History of the Civil War. 3 vols.: The Coming Fury, Terrible Swift Sword, Never Call Retreat.* Garden City, N.Y.: Doubleday, 1961–65.

———. *A Stillness at Appomattox.* Garden City, N.Y.: Doubleday, 1953.

Foote, Shelby. *The Civil War: A Narrative. Vols. 1–3.* New York: Random House, 1958–74.

Ketchum, Richard M., ed. *American Heritage Picture History of the Civil War.* New York: American Heritage Publishing, 1960.

McPherson, James M. *Battle Cry of Freedom: The Civil War Era.* New York: Oxford University Press, 1988.

———. *Ordeal by Fire: The Civil War and Reconstruction.* New York: McGraw-Hill, 1992.

Symonds, Craig L. *A Battlefield Atlas of the Civil War.* Cartography by William J. Clipson. Baltimore: Nautical and Aviation Pub. Co. of America, 1993.

Books about the events leading to the Civil War

After working through the books covering the entire Civil War, I looked for books that would tell me about events that led up to it. These were some helpful sources. Anyone who thinks politics is hopelessly partisan and mean today should look back at just how nasty things got in the 1850s!

Bordewich, Fergus M. *Bound for Canaan: The Epic Story of the Underground Railroad.* New York: HarperCollins, 2005.

Johannsen, Robert W., ed. *The Lincoln-Douglas Debates of 1858.* New York: Oxford University Press, 1965.

Klein, Maury. *Days of Defiance: Sumter, Secession, and the Coming of the Civil War.* New York: Alfred A. Knopf, 1997.

Miller, Marion Mills, ed. *Great Debates in American History. Vol. 4.* New York: Current Literature Pub. Co., 1913.

Oates, Stephen. *To Purge This Land with Blood.* New York: Harper & Row, 1970.

Potter, David Morris. *The Impending Crisis, 1848–1861.* New York: Harper & Row, 1976.

Schlesinger, Arthur M. *Congress Investigates: A Documentary History.* New York: Chelsea House, 1975.

Stowe, Harriet Beecher. *Uncle Tom's Cabin.* New York: Modern Library, 1938.

Books and articles about specific Civil War battles or subjects

After making an outline for the book, I started looking for great stories and quotes for each chapter. There's no shortage of material—more than 50,000 books have been written about various Civil War subjects! No, I didn't read all of them. I focused on the books below, because they give readers great real-life details about what it was like to live through these events.

Bailey, Ronald H. *The Bloodiest Day: The Battle of Antietam.* Alexandria, Va.: Time-Life Books, 1984.

———. *Forward to Richmond: McClellan's Peninsular Campaign.* Alexandria, Va.: Time-Life Books, 1983.

Bennett, Lerone. "Chronicles of Black Courage: African American Confederate Sailor Robert Smalls." *Ebony,* Nov. 2001.

Block, Eugene. *Above the Civil War: The Story of Thaddeus Lowe.* Berkeley, Calif.: Howell-North Books, 1966.

Channing, Steven A. *Confederate Ordeal: The Southern Home Front.* Alexandria, Va.: Time-Life Books, 1984.

Clark, Champ. *Gettysburg: The Confederate High Tide.* Alexandria, Va.: Time-Life Books, 1985.

Daniel, Larry J. *Shiloh: The Battle That Changed the Civil War.* New York: Simon & Schuster, 1997.

Davis, William C. *Death in the Trenches: Grant at Petersburg.* Alexandria, Va.: Time-Life Books, 1986.

Furgurson, Ernest B. *Not War but Murder: Cold Harbor, 1864.* New York: Alfred A. Knopf, 2000.

Goolrick, William K. *Rebels Resurgent: Fredericksburg to Chancellorsville.* Alexandria, Va.: Time-Life Books, 1985.

Hoehling, A. A. *Vicksburg: Forty-seven Days of Siege.* Englewood Cliffs, N.J.: Prentice-Hall, 1969.

Horigan, Michael. *Elmira: Death Camp of the North.* Mechanicsburg, Pa.: Stackpole Books, 2002.

Kane, Harnett Thomas. *Spies for the Blue and Gray.* Garden City, N.Y.: Hanover House, 1954.

Korn, Jerry. *The Fight for Chattanooga: Chickamauga to Missionary Ridge.* Alexandria, Va.: Time-Life Books, 1985.

———. *War on the Mississippi: Grant's Vicksburg Campaign.* Alexandria, Va.: Time-Life Books, 1985.

Lawson, John D., ed. *American State Trials. Vol. 13.* St. Louis: Thomas Law Book Company, 1921.

McPherson, *James M. Crossroads of Freedom: Antietam.* New York: Oxford University Press, 2002.

Nevin, David. *Sherman's March: Atlanta to the Sea.* Alexandria, Va.: Time-Life Books, 1986.

Trudeau, Noah Andre. *Gettysburg: A Testing of Courage.* New York: HarperCollins, 2002.

Winik, Jay. *April 1865: The Month That Saved America.* New York: HarperCollins, 2001.

Biographies of major Civil War figures

The Civil War has a cast of characters no writer could invent—including the one who gets my personal vote for the best character in American history: Abraham Lincoln. Sometimes I'll read entire biographies in search of just one or two interesting details to help bring the character to life. (Well, maybe I don't always read the entire book.)

Clinton, Catherine. *Harriet Tubman: The Road to Freedom.* Boston: Little, Brown, 2004.

Davis, Burke. *J.E.B. Stuart: The Last Cavalier.* New York, Rinehart, 1957.

Davis, William C. *Jefferson Davis: The Man and His Hour.* New York: HarperCollins, 1991.

Douglass, Frederick. *Life and Times of Frederick Douglass.* Boston: De Wolfe & Fiske Co., 1892.

———. *Narrative of the Life of Frederick Douglass, an American Slave.* Boston: Dublin, Webb and Chapman, 1846.

Fellman, Michael. *Citizen Sherman: A Life of William Tecumseh Sherman.* New York: Random House, 1995.

Freeman, Douglas Southall. *R. E. Lee: A Biography.* New York: C. Scribner's Sons, 1934.

Hedrick, Joan D. *Harriet Beecher Stowe: A Life.* New York: Oxford University Press, 1994.

Johnston, Richard Malcolm, and William Browne. *Alexander Stephens.* Philadelphia: J. B. Lippincott & Co., 1878.

Larson, Kate Clifford. *Bound for the Promised Land: Harriet Tubman, Portrait of an American Hero.* New York: Ballantine, 2004.

Oates, Stephen B. *Abraham Lincoln: The Man Behind the Myths.* New York: Harper & Row, 1984.

Perret, Geoffrey. *Ulysses S. Grant: Soldier and President.* New York: Random House, 1997.

Ross, Ishbel. *First Lady of the South.* New York: Harper, 1985.

Sandburg, Carl. *Abraham Lincoln: The Prairie Years and the War Years.* 1-vol. ed. New York: Harcourt, Brace & World, 1954.

Sears, Stephen W. *George B. McClellan: The Young Napoleon.* New York: Ticknor & Fields, 1988.

Simpson, Brooks D. *Ulysses S. Grant: Triumph over Adversity, 1822–1865.* Boston: Houghton Mifflin, 2000.

Wells, Damon. *Stephen Douglas: The Last Years, 1857–1861.* Austin: University of Texas Press, 1971.

Books about everyday life for soldiers and civilians

I think the everyday men and women in history are at least as interesting as the famous guys—and often much more interesting. These books give us an inside look at what life was really like for the people who fought in the Civil War. If I had to pick just two, I'd probably take the Bell Irvin Wiley books, which are gold mines of amazing details you'd never find in textbooks.

Blanton, DeAnne, and Cook, Lauren M. *They Fought Like Demons: Women Soldiers in the American Civil War.* Baton Rouge: Louisiana State University Press, 2002.

Botkin, B.A. *Civil War Treasury of Tales, Legends, and Folklore.* New York: Random House: 1960.

Cornish, Dudley Taylor. *The Sable Arm: Black Troops in the Union Army, 1861–1865.* Lawrence: University Press of Kansas, 1987.

Gansler, Laura L. *The Mysterious Private Thompson: The Double Life of Sarah Emma Edmonds, Civil War Soldier.* New York: Free Press, 2005.

Ochs, Stephen. *A Black Patriot and a White Priest: Andre Cailloux and Claude Paschal Maistre in Civil War New Orleans.* Baton Rouge: Louisiana State University Press, 2000.

Pullen, John J. *The Twentieth Maine: A Volunteer Regiment in the Civil War.* Philadelphia: Lippincott, 1957.

Trudeau, Noah Andre. *Like Men of War: Black Troops in the Civil War, 1862–1865.* Boston: Little, Brown, 1998.

Uya, Okon Edet. *Robert Smalls: From Slavery to Public Service, 1839–1915.* New York: Oxford University Press, 1971.

Wiley, Bell Irvin, *The Life of Billy Yank.* New York: Grosset & Dunlap, 1958.

———. *The Life of Johnny Reb.* New York: Grosset & Dunlap, 1958.

Collections of primary sources from the Civil War

Of course, the best way to find out what life was like during a certain time in history is to read stories told by the people who were actually there. These books collect quotes from Civil War participants, organizing them by subject. *The Blue and the Gray* is an especially incredible resource—more than 1,100 pages of quotes, and none of them boring!

Commanger, Henry Steele. *The Blue and the Gray: The Story of the Civil War as Told by Participants*. Indianapolis: Bobbs-Merrill, 1950.

Voices of the Civil War: Antietam. By the editors of Time-Life Books. Alexandria, Va.: Time-Life Books, 1996.

Voices of the Civil War: Chancellorsville. By the editors of Time-Life Books. Alexandria, Va.: Time-Life Books, 1996.

Voices of the Civil War: Gettysburg. By the editors of Time-Life Books. Alexandria, Va.: Time-Life Books, 1995.

Voices of the Civil War: Soldier Life. By the editors of Time-Life Books. Alexandria, Va.: Time-Life Books, 1996.

Wheeler, Richard. *Voices of the Civil War.* New York: Crowell, 1976.

Memoirs and writings by Civil War figures and participants

Lots of men and women kept journals and diaries during the Civil War, which is great news for writers and readers today. These books give us close-up looks at the war from all different points of view. Just how disgusting was everyday life in army camps? How tough was it to stay alive in a prisoner of war camp? Exactly how did women get away with disguising themselves as men and joining the army? What was Abraham Lincoln really like when he wasn't giving famous speeches? You'll find answers to these and many other burning questions in the books below.

Alleman, Tillie Pierce. *At Gettysburg; or, What a Girl Saw and Heard of The Battle.* New York: W. L. Borland, 1889.

Andrews, Eliza Frances. *The War-Time Journal of a Georgia Girl, 1864–1865.* New York: D. Appleton and Company, 1908.

Billings, John Davis. *Hardtack and Coffee; or, The Unwritten Story of Army Life.* Boston: G.M. Smith & Co., 1887.

Boyd, Belle. *Belle Boyd in Camp and Prison.* London: Saunders, Otley, and Co., 1865.

Burge, Dolly Lunt. *A Woman's Wartime Journal: An Account of the Passage over Georgia's Plantation of Sherman's Army on the March to the Sea.* New York: Century Co., 1918.

Carpenter, F. B. *Six Months at the White House.* New York: Hurd and Houghton, 1866.

Chamberlain, Joshua Lawrence. *Through Blood and Fire: Selected Civil War Papers of Major General Joshua Chamberlain.* Edited by Mark Nesbitt. Mechanicsburg, Pa.: Stackpole Books, 1996.

Chesnut, Mary Boykin. *A Diary from Dixie.* New York: D. Appleton & Company, 1905.

Edmonds, S. Emma. *Nurse and Spy in the Union Army: Comprising the Adventures and Experiences of a Woman in Hospitals, Camps and Battlefields.* Hartford, Conn.: W. S. Williams, 1865.

Grant, Ulysses S. *Personal Memoirs of U. S. Grant.* New York: Modern Library, 1999.

Haskell, Frank. *The Battle of Gettysburg.* Boston: Mudge Press, 1908.

Jones, John Beauchamp. *A Rebel War Clerk's Diary.* Philadelphia: Lippincott, 1866.

Lee, Robert, E. *The Wartime Papers of Robert E. Lee.* Edited by Clifford Dowdey. Boston: Little, Brown, 1961.

Lincoln, Abraham. *The Life and Writings of Abraham Lincoln.* Edited by Phillip Van Doren Stern. New York: Modern Library, 1999.

———. *Lincoln: His Speeches and Writings.* Edited by Roy Prentice Basler. Cambridge, Mass.: Da Capo Press, 2001.

———. *The Lincoln Reader.* Edited by Paul M. Angle. New Brunswick, N.J.: Rutgers University Press, 1947.

———. *Speeches and Writings, 1832–1858.* New York: Library of America, 1989.

Longstreet, James. "Lee's Right Wing at Gettysburg." In *Battles and Leaders of the Civil War, Vol. 3.* Edited by Robert Underwood Johnson. New York: Yoseloff, 1956.

Loughborough, Mary Ann Webster. *My Cave Life in Vicksburg, with Letters of Trial and Travel.* New York: D. Appleton and Company, 1864.

McCarthy, Carlton. *Detailed Minutiae of Soldier Life in the Army of Northern Virginia, 1861–1865.* Richmond: C. McCarthy and Co., 1882.

McClellan, George B. *McCelllan's Own Story.* New York: Charles L. Webster & Co., 1886.

Myers, Elizabeth. "How a Gettysburg Schoolteacher Spent Her Vacation in 1863." *Philadelphia North American,* July 4, 1909.

Perry, John Gardner. *Letters from a Surgeon of the Civil War.* Boston: Little, Brown, 1906.

Ramsay, H. Ashton. "The Most Famous of Sea Duels." *Harper's Weekly,* February 10, 1912.

Ransom, John L. *Andersonville Diary; Escape, and List of Dead.* Philadelphia: Douglass Bros., 1883.

Seward, William H. *The Works of William H. Seward.* Edited by George E. Baker. New York: Redfield, 1853.

Sumner, Charles. *Works of Charles Sumner.* Boston: Lee and Shepard, 1875.

Velazquez, Loreta Janeta. *The Woman in Battle: A Narrative of the Exploits, Adventures, and Travels of Madame Loreta Janeta Velazquez.* Richmond: Dustin, Gilman & Co., 1876.

Watkins, Samuel R. *"Co. Aytch": First Tennessee Regiment; or, A Side Show of the Big Show.* Nashville: Cumberland Presbyterian Publishing House, 1882.

Young, Jesse. *What a Boy Saw in the Army.* New York: Hunt & Eaton, 1894.

Zettler, Berrian McPherson. *War Stories and School-Day Incidents.* New York: Neale Publishing Co., 1912.

Quotation Notes

Why are textbooks so boring? I could explain—but it would be boring. I'll just mention one serious problem with textbooks: they always seem to avoid quotes that are at all funny, amazing, surprising, disgusting, confusing, stupid, mean, or anything else interesting. One of my main goals with this book was to fill it with all the quotes I never got to use in textbooks. Just in case you think I made some of this stuff up, here's a list of the sources where the quotes can be found. For more information about the sources, look in the Source Notes.

How to Rip a Country Apart

"One man will clean ten times as much cotton" Bordewich, *Bound for Canaan.*
"Why am I a slave?" Douglass, *Narrative of the Life of Frederick Douglass.*
"Who saw this assault" Douglass, *Narrative of the Life.*
"Had the conductor looked closely" Douglass, *Life and Times of Frederick Douglass.*
"I found myself in the big city" Douglass, *Life and Times.*
"When I found I had crossed" Bordewich, *Bound for Canaan.*
"For the first time, we are about to" McPherson, *Battle Cry of Freedom.*
"The South asks for justice" Miller, *Great Debates.*
"I cannot consent to introduce slavery" Seward, *Works of William H. Seward.*
"I have no pistols!" Chambers, *U.S. Senate records, April 3, 1850.*
"I wish to speak today" *U.S. Senate records, March 7, 1850.*
"The Union is saved!" McPherson, *Battle Cry.*
"If it were your Harry, mother" Stowe, *Uncle Tom's Cabin.*
"There can be no moral right" Lincoln, *Speeches and Writings.*
"When the white man governs himself" Lincoln, *Speeches and Writings.*
"There are eleven hundred men" McPherson, *Battle Cry.*
"STARTLING NEWS FROM KANSAS" Potter, *Impending Crisis.*
"murderous robbers from Missouri" Sumner, *Works of Charles Sumner.*
"I have read your speech twice over" Sumner, *Works of Charles Sumner.*
"Every Southern man is delighted" McPherson, *Ordeal by Fire.*

John Brown Lights the Fuse

"became considerably excited" Oates, *To Purge This Land.*
"I hope you will act with caution" Oates, *To Purge This Land.*
"What is it?" Oates, *To Purge This Land.*
"Believing that under this state of fact" Lawson, *American State Trials.*
"no rights which the white man" McPherson, *Ordeal by Fire.*
"I have really got it into my head" Sandburg, *Abraham Lincoln.*
"The things I want to know" Sandburg, *Abraham Lincoln.*
"He can sink an axe deeper" Foote, *Civil War, vol. 1.*
"I never saw a more thoughtful face" Sandburg, *Abraham Lincoln.*
"Abraham Lincoln is the first" Johannsen, *Lincoln-Douglas Debates.*
"You have nominated a very able" Wells, *Stephen Douglas.*
"A house divided against itself" Lincoln, *Speeches and Writings.*
"Put on your specs!" Johannsen, *Lincoln-Douglas Debates.*
"Let each state mind its own business" Johannsen, *Lincoln-Douglas Debates.*
"If slavery is not wrong" Johannsen, *Lincoln-Douglas Debates.*
"That is the real issue" Johannsen, *Lincoln-Douglas Debates.*
"Mary insists that I am going to be" Sandburg, *Abraham Lincoln.*
"Dear Husband . . ." Oates, *To Purge This Land.*
"What was your object in coming?" Oates, *To Purge This Land.*
"I John Brown am now" McPherson, *Ordeal by Fire.*
"to incite slaves to murder" Potter, *Impending Crisis.*
"THE DAY OF COMPROMISE" McPherson, *Ordeal by Fire.*
"Never before, since the Declaration" Potter, *Impending Crisis.*
"The only persons who do not" Potter, *Impending Crisis.*
"What right of yours, gentlemen" McPherson, *Ordeal by Fire.*
"What do you think of matters" Johnston, *Alexander Stephens.*
"A herd of buffaloes" McPherson, *Battle Cry.*
"Well, gentlemen, there is a short woman" Lincoln, *Lincoln Reader.*
"Ain't you glad you joined" McPherson, *Battle Cry.*
"there will have to be a separation" Klein, *Days of Defiance.*

Abe Lincoln's Troublesome Victory

"Lincoln's elected" Chesnut, *Diary from Dixie.*
"Mary, we're elected" Sandburg, *Abraham Lincoln.*
"We are either slaves in the Union" McPherson, *Battle Cry.*
"I am the last president" Lincoln, *Life and Writings.*
"I would prefer not to have" Davis, *Jefferson Davis.*

"Sir: We are directed to" Foote, *Civil War, vol. 1.*
"as a man might speak of" Foote, *Civil War, vol. 1.*
"I will do my best" Davis, *Jefferson Davis.*
"The South is determined" McPherson, *Battle Cry.*
"I am sick of office-holding already" Foote, *Civil War, vol. 1.*
"My father is going to vote for you" Lincoln, *Speeches and Writings.*
"I have a correspondent" Sandburg, *Abraham Lincoln.*
"In your hands, my dissatisfied" Lincoln, *Speeches and Writings.*
"Why did that green goose Anderson" Chesnut, *Diary from Dixie.*
"I do not pretend to sleep" Chesnut, *Diary from Dixie.*
"The scene at this time was" Commanger, *Blue and the Gray.*
"The rebs have fired" Commanger, *Blue and the Gray.*
"Death to traitors!" McPherson, *Battle Cry.*
"We shall crush out this rebellion" Sandburg, *Abraham Lincoln.*
"Tennessee will furnish not a single man" McPherson, *Battle Cry.*
"So impatient did I become" Wiley, *Life of Johnny Reb.*
"If a fellow wants to go with a girl now" Wiley, *Life of Billy Yank.*
"The women of the South generally" Commanger, *Blue and the Gray.*
"I wish that women could fight" Blanton and Cook, *They Fought Like Demons.*
"Our mothers—God bless them" Commanger, *Blue and the Gray.*
"Well, Mary, the question is settled" Freeman, *R. E. Lee.*
"the very best soldier I ever saw" Lee, *Wartime Papers.*
"I could take no part in an invasion" Lee, *Wartime Papers.*
"You must think as kindly" Lee, *Wartime Papers.*
"Old Abe has his legs" Sandburg, *Abraham Lincoln.*
"monstrous fine!" Foote, *Civil War, vol. 1.*
"You are green, it is true" McPherson, *Ordeal by Fire.*
"McDowell has certainly been" Kane, *Spies for the Blue and Gray.*
"That is splendid! Oh, my!" Commanger, *Blue and the Gray.*

This Is Going to Be Serious

"Remember, boys, battle and fighting" Zettler, *War Stories.*
"The boys dropped from the apple tree" Zettler, *War Stories.*
"If my hair at that moment" Zettler, *War Stories.*
"No one can see a battle" Zettler, *War Stories.*
"Didn't I tell you so?" McPherson, *Battle Cry.*
"Steady, men. All's well." Foote, *Civil War, vol. 1.*
"Look! There is Jackson" McPherson, *Ordeal by Fire.*

"And when you charge" Foote, *Civil War, vol. 1.*
"What is the matter, sir?" Commanger, *Blue and the Gray.*
"We have taught them a lesson" Davis, *Jefferson Davis.*
"Who would have thought" McClellan, *McClellan's Own Story.*
"You have no idea how the men" McClellan, *McClellan's Own Story.*
"The president is nothing more" McPherson, *Battle Cry.*
"I will hold McClellan's horse" McPherson, *Battle Cry.*
"You're Mrs. Greenhow?" Kane, *Spies.*
"What can I do?" Gansler, *Private Thompson.*
"You have pretty good health" Wiley, *Billy Yank.*
"I was perfectly wild on the subject" Velazquez, *Woman in Battle.*
"My husband's farewell kisses" Velazquez, *Woman in Battle.*
"This is the kind of fellow we want" Velazquez, *Woman in Battle.*
"To say that I was frightened" Velazquez, *Woman in Battle.*
"It is hard, hard, hard" Sandburg, *Abraham Lincoln.*
"We were met by a storm of shells" Ramsay, *Sea Duels.*
"We thought at first it was a raft" McPherson, *Battle Cry.*
"We of the *Monitor* thought, and still think" Commanger, *Blue and the Gray.*
"I would have given anything then" Grant, *Personal Memoirs.*
"It occurred to me at once" Grant, *Personal Memoirs.*
"No terms except unconditional" Catton, *Terrible Swift Sword.*
"an expression as if he had determined" Ketchum, *Picture History.*
"We have recently met with" McPherson, *Battle Cry.*
"Good-bye. If I do not write" Daniel, *Shiloh.*
"I may run" Wiley, *Johnny Reb.*
"I have a mortal dread" Wiley, *Billy Yank.*
"I have ordered a battle" Catton, *Terrible Swift Sword.*
"The rebels are coming" Foote, *Civil War, vol. 1.*
"Just look at that brave man" Watkins, *"Co. Aytch."*
"Everywhere it was one never-ending" Ketchum, *Picture History.*
"I will lead you!" Foote, *Civil War, vol. 1.*
"General, are you hurt?" Foote, *Civil War, vol. 1.*
"Well, Grant, we've had the devil's" Simpson, *Ulysses S. Grant.*

Two Miserable Presidents

"I can't spare this man" McPherson, *Battle Cry.*
"Oh! How I hate the Yankees!" Catton, *Terrible Swift Sword.*
"He's got the slows." Sandburg, *Abraham Lincoln.*

"Oh, mother, Uncle Jeff is miserable." McPherson, *Crossroads of Freedom.*
"I wish I could learn just to let" Foote, *Civil War, vol. 1.*
"Jefferson Davis now treats all men" Foote, *Civil War, vol. 1.*
"The enemy greatly outnumber" Catton, *Never Call Retreat.*
"He could sleep in any position" Commanger, *Blue and the Gray.*
"Hello! I say, old fellow" Commanger, *Blue and the Gray.*
"Men, every member of this household" Boyd, *Belle Boyd.*
"I could stand it no longer" Boyd, *Belle Boyd.*
"No, no. You go." Boyd, *Belle Boyd.*
"The rifle-balls flew thick and fast" Boyd, *Belle Boyd.*
"MISS BELLE BOYD: I thank you" Boyd, *Belle Boyd.*
"You must act." Catton, *Terrible Swift Sword.*
"The time is very near" Catton, *Terrible Swift Sword.*
"Open the valve!" Block, *Above the Civil War.*
"How do you feel, boys?" Foote, *Civil War, vol. 1.*
"He will take more chances" McPherson, *Ordeal by Fire.*
"And if I find the way open" Davis, *J.E.B. Stuart.*
"Come on, come on, my men!" Sandburg, *Abraham Lincoln.*
"Our boys and the Yanks" McPherson, *Ordeal by Fire.*
"McClellan has the army" McPherson, *Ordeal by Fire.*
"To fight against slaveholders" McPherson, *Battle Cry.*
"I can assure you that the subject" Foote, *Civil War, vol. 1.*
"In the matter of rights" McPherson, *Ordeal by Fire.*
"I have the honor, sir" Bennett, *"Chronicles."*
"Well, John, we are whipped again" Foote, *Civil War, vol. 1.*
"The army is not properly equipped." Bailey, *Bloodiest Day.*
"the dirtiest men I ever saw" Ketchum, *Picture History.*
"As I read, each line became" McPherson, *Crossroads of Freedom.*
"Here is a paper with which" Ketchum, *Picture History.*
"We will make our stand" McPherson, *Crossroads of Freedom.*
"I have never seen a more disgusted" McPherson, *Crossroads of Freedom.*
"Every one dropped whatever he had" *Voices: Antietam.*
"Fragments of the poor fellow's head" *Voices: Antietam.*
"A savage continual thunder" Wiley, *Billy Yank.*
"The earth and sky seemed" *Voices: Antietam.*
"It seemed as if a million bees" *Voices: Antietam.*
"the awful tornado of battle." Bailey, *Bloodiest Day.*
"I have never mended" *Voices: Antietam.*
"The enemy is driven back" Catton, *Terrible Swift Sword.*
"Will you pardon me for asking" McPherson, *Ordeal by Fire.*

"There never was a truer epithet." McPherson, *Ordeal by Fire.*
"I think the time has come." McPherson, *Crossroads of Freedom.*
"On the first day of January" Lincoln, *Speeches and Writings.*

Johnny Reb vs. Billy Yank

"Get your guns!" Commanger, *Blue and the Gray.*
"Good heavens, Billy" Commanger, *Blue and the Gray.*
"I caught sight of that half-shaved" Commanger, *Blue and the Gray.*
"All right, Bob" Commanger, *Blue and the Gray.*
"He began to call Hunter" Commanger, *Blue and the Gray.*
"Why, Bob" Commanger, *Blue and the Gray.*
"To be one day without" McCarthy, *Detailed Minutiae.*
"The beef is so poor" Wiley, *Johnny Reb.*
"Very few of us knew" Commanger, *Blue and the Gray.*
"I found what I supposed" *Voices: Soldier Life.*
"Once I took some corn" Wiley, *Johnny Reb.*
"We had fifteen different ways" *Voices: Soldier Life.*
"It was no uncommon occurrence" Billings, *Hardtack and Coffee.*
"No-siree-bob!" Kane, *Spies.*
"Johnny Reb! I say, Johnny Reb" Commanger, *Blue and the Gray.*
"Gents, U.S. Army" Wiley, *Billy Yank.*
"What luck some people have" Catton, *Never Call Retreat.*
"If I fall, never mind me" Goolrick, *Rebels Resurgent.*
"My mouth was full of blood" Goolrick, *Rebels Resurgent.*
"At this time there was no one" Commanger, *Blue and the Gray.*
"It is well that war is so terrible" Ketchum, *Picture History.*
"Oh, those men! Those men" Ketchum, *Picture History.*
"There was a hospital within thirty" Wiley, *Billy Yank.*
"We operated in old blood-stained" Wiley, *Billy Yank.*
"On rolling up my bed" Wiley, *Johnny Reb.*
"smells so offensively that the men" Wiley, *Johnny Reb.*
"There are two brothers who are" *Voices: Soldier Life.*
"I am without drawers " Wiley, *Johnny Reb.*
"at least once a week" *Voices: Soldier Life.*
"We are now on the brink of destruction" McPherson, *Ordeal by Fire.*
"My plans are perfect" Wheeler, *Voices.*
"That is the most depressing thing" Goolrick, *Rebels Resurgent.*
"It must be victory or death" *Voices: Chancellorsville.*

"Press on, press forward!" Goolrick, *Rebels Resurgent.*
"Well to tell the truth, I just lost" Wheeler, *Voices.*
"The woods around the house were" *Voices: Chancellorsville.*
"At Chancellorsville we gained another" Goolrick, *Rebels Resurgent.*
"He has lost his left arm" McPherson, *Ordeal by Fire.*
"His fearful wounds, his mutilated arm" *Voices: Chancellorsville.*
"Doctor, Anna informs me that" *Voices: Chancellorsville.*
"Order A. P. Hill to prepare" Wheeler, *Voices.*
"Never, as long as I knew him" Lincoln, *Lincoln Reader.*
"My God! My God! What will the country" Lincoln, *Lincoln Reader.*
"Well, then, will you lend me five dollars?" Sandburg, *Abraham Lincoln.*
"What do you want me to do?" Sandburg, *Abraham Lincoln.*
"General, I'm afraid I've come" Foote, *Civil War, vol. 2.*
"We crossed the line" Commanger, *Blue and the Gray.*

The Second-Biggest Fourth of July

"Yes, we'll rally round the flag" Wheeler, *Voices.*
"Many strong men wept" Wheeler, *Voices.*
"General Lee said that he really had none" *Voices: Gettysburg.*
"Hello, my little Yank" Wheeler, *Voices.*
"held the South's two halves" Foote, *Civil War, vol. 2.*
"I think Grant has hardly a friend" McPherson, *Ordeal by Fire.*
"I was now in the enemy's country" McPherson, *Ordeal by Fire.*
"a very determined little fellow." Commanger, *Blue and the Gray.*
"Mississippians don't know, and refuse" McPherson, *Battle Cry.*
"If the world doubts our fighting" Trudeau, *Men of War.*
"I will bring back these colors" Ochs, *Black Patriot.*
"They charged and re-charged" Trudeau, *Men of War.*
"They fought splendidly." Trudeau, *Men of War.*
"Rats, of which there were plenty" Commanger, *Blue and the Gray.*
"They flop up and down" Wiley, *Johnny Reb.*
"If there is no objection, I will take" Foote, *Civil War, vol. 2.*
"Children, run home" Alleman, *At Gettysburg.*
"Some of the girls did not reach" Alleman, *At Gettysburg.*
"Tell Lee to hold on just a little" Trudeau, *Gettysburg.*
"I thought some of the boys" Wheeler, *Voices.*
"I can get my hands in here" Wheeler, *Voices.*
"The fate of the nation" Trudeau, *Gettysburg.*
"I think this is the strongest position" Foote, *Civil War, vol. 2.*

"No, the enemy is there" Foote, *Civil War, vol. 2.*
"I am glad to hear you say so" Foote, *Civil War, vol. 2.*
"This is the turning point" Young, *What a Boy Saw.*
"This is the left of the Union line" Pullen, *Twentieth Maine.*
"Boys, I don't like this" Pullen, *Twentieth Maine.*
"Some of my men fainted" Commanger, *Blue and the Gray.*
"How can I describe" Commanger, *Blue and the Gray.*
"At times I saw around" Pullen, *Twentieth Maine.*
"My dead and wounded" Wheeler, *Voices.*
"As a last, desperate resort" Chamberlain, *Blood and Fire.*
"We struck them with" Pullen, *Twentieth Maine.*
"There never were harder fighters" Commanger, *Blue and the Gray.*
"The first wounded soldier whom" Alleman, *At Gettysburg.*
"I never could bear the sight" Myers, *Gettysburg Schoolteacher.*
"There were never such men" Sandburg, *Abraham Lincoln.*
"We are utterly cut off" Commanger, *Blue and the Gray.*
"Cave-digging has become" Commanger, *Blue and the Gray.*
"We were almost eaten up" Commanger, *Blue and the Gray.*
"Terror stricken, we remained" Loughborough, *Cave Life.*
"We expected every moment" Loughborough, *Cave Life.*
"The cheeks became thin" Hoehling, *Vicksburg.*
"Mother would not eat mule" Hoehling, *Vicksburg.*
"If you can't feed us" McPherson, *Battle Cry.*
"I have been a soldier" Longstreet, *"Lee's Right Wing."*
"The enemy is there" Longstreet, *"Lee's Right Wing."*
"the hottest day I think I ever saw." *Voices: Gettysburg.*
"Up, men, and to your posts!" Commanger, *Blue and the Gray.*
"No man who looked on" Young, *What a Boy Saw.*
"Hold your position, don't fire" *Voices: Gettysburg.*
"Come on, Johnny!" Foote, *Civil War, vol. 2.*
"Arms, heads, blankets, guns" *Clark, Gettysburg.*
"At every step some poor fellow" *Voices: Gettysburg.*
"It's all my fault." Foote, *Civil War, vol. 2.*
"Some cried, others shook hands" *Voices: Gettysburg.*
"We are now in the darkest hour" *Foote, Civil War, vol. 2.*
"I cannot, in words" Sandburg, *Abraham Lincoln.*
"Peace does not appear so" Commanger, *Blue and the Gray.*

Can Anyone Win This War?

"A Confederate soldier captured eight" Wiley, *Johnny Reb.*
"We had them in our grasp" McPherson, *Ordeal by Fire.*
"I'm a tired man" Sandburg, *Abraham Lincoln.*
"For ninety-six hours" Catton, *Never Call Retreat.*
"The whole of the army" Commanger, *Blue and the Gray.*
"Will no one have mercy" Wiley, *Johnny Reb.*
"Stop! Oh! For God's sake" Wiley, *Johnny Reb.*
"I sensibly feel the growing" Lee, *Wartime Papers.*
"Our country could not bear" Commanger, *Blue and the Gray.*
"My God! How can I pay" McPherson, *Ordeal by Fire.*
"Some had hatchets" Channing, *Confederate Ordeal.*
"We are starving" McPherson, *Battle Cry.*
"Here is all I have" Channing, *Confederate Ordeal.*
"My friends, you have one" McPherson, *Battle Cry.*
"I heard loud and continued cheers" Perry, *Letters from a Surgeon.*
"A rich man's war" McPherson, *Ordeal by Fire.*
"Colonel Montgomery and his gallant" Clinton, *Harriet Tubman.*
"Women would come with twins" Clinton, *Harriet Tubman.*
"I made up my mind then" Larson, *Bound for the Promised Land.*
"Every black man and woman" Trudeau, *Men of War.*
"Men fell all around me" Trudeau, *Men of War.*
"In this position I remained" Trudeau, *Men of War.*
"And the officer in charge said" Trudeau, *Men of War.*
"This year has brought" McPherson, *Ordeal by Fire.*
"Fourscore and seven years" Lincoln, *Speeches and Writings.*
"Lamon, that speech" Sandburg, *Abraham Lincoln.*
"They have fought their last man" Korn, *Fight for Chattanooga.*
"He was an expert drummer" Korn, *Fight for Chattanooga.*
"I did not like to stand" Wiley, *Billy Yank.*
"Surrender, you little Yankee!" Wiley, *Billy Yank.*
"This announcement has lifted" Jones, *A Rebel War Clerk's Diary.*
"confused and stunned" Sandburg, *Abraham Lincoln.*
"Thomas, who ordered" McPherson, *Ordeal by Fire.*
"Bragg's disaster so shocked" Jones, *A Rebel War Clerk's Diary.*
"My heart aches." McPherson, *Ordeal by Fire.*
"Nothing can be worse" Ransom, *Andersonville Diary.*
"Could die in two hours" Ransom, *Andersonville Diary.*
"When ready to change" Commanger, *Blue and the Gray.*

"We thought we could dig" Horigan, *Elmira.*
"Half past three o'clock" Horigan, *Elmira.*
"I have the honor to inform you" Perret, *Ulysses S. Grant.*
"It is General Grant" Simpson, *Ulysses S. Grant.*
"Stand up so we can all" Perret, *Ulysses S. Grant.*
"Really, Mr. Lincoln" Foote, *Civil War, vol. 3.*
"I must have this day" Foote, *Civil War, vol. 3.*
"We have got to whip" Foote, *Civil War, vol. 3.*
"That man will fight us" Foote, *Civil War, vol. 3.*

The Bloody Road to Richmond

"He was to go for Lee" Foote, *Civil War, vol. 3.*
"hammer continuously against" Foote, *Civil War, vol. 3.*
"No one could see the fight" Commanger, *Blue and the Gray.*
"You Yanks don't call this" Commanger, *Blue and the Gray.*
"The men fought the enemy" Commanger, *Blue and the Gray.*
"Our spirits rose" Foote, *Civil War, vol. 3.*
"If you see the president" Perret, *Ulysses S. Grant.*
"General Grant will not retreat" Botkin, *Civil War Treasury.*
"General Lee to the rear!" Commanger, *Blue and the Gray.*
"If you will promise me" Foote, *Civil War, vol. 3.*
"I never expect to be" McPherson, *Ordeal by Fire.*
"Lee's army is really whipped." McPherson, *Battle Cry.*
"The men were calmly writing" Foote, *Civil War, vol. 3.*
"June 3, 1864. Cold Harbor" McPherson, *Ordeal by Fire.*
"We started with a yell" Furguson, *Not War but Murder.*
"To your guns, boys" Furguson, *Not War but Murder.*
"It seemed more like a volcanic" Foote, *Civil War, vol. 3.*
"The dead covered five acres" Commanger, *Blue and the Gray.*
"I regret this assault more" McPherson, *Battle Cry.*
"They call me a butcher." Perret, *Ulysses S. Grant.*
"You could put a piece" Foote, *Civil War, vol. 3.*
"There were days when I could" Carpenter, *Six Months.*
"Mr. President, you are standing" Botkin, *Civil War Treasury.*
"We could blow that fort" McPherson, *Ordeal by Fire.*
"Suddenly the earth trembled" Commanger, *Blue and the Gray.*
"the saddest affair I have" McPherson, *Ordeal by Fire.*
"What is all this struggling" Commanger, *Blue and the Gray.*
"Lincoln is deader than dead." McPherson, *Ordeal by Fire.*

"I told Mr. Lincoln" Sandburg, *Abraham Lincoln.*
"I am going to be beaten" McPherson, *Battle Cry.*
"The most restless man" Botkin, *Civil War Treasury.*
"Atlanta is ours, and fairly won." McPherson, *Ordeal by Fire.*
"Since Atlanta I have felt" Chesnut, *Diary from Dixie.*
"You know, that reminds me" Carpenter, Six Months.
"I had rather stay out here" McPherson, *Ordeal by Fire.*
"Say, Yank!" McPherson, *Ordeal by Fire.*
"We will be free" McPherson, *Battle Cry.*
"Like demons they rush in!" Burge, *Woman's Wartime Journal.*
"I can make the march" McPherson, *Ordeal by Fire.*
"War is cruelty" Foote, *Civil War, vol. 3.*
"We will hang Jeff Davis" Nevin, *Sherman's March.*
"The stench in some places" Andrews, *War-Time Journal*
"I beg to present you" McPherson, *Battle Cry.*
"We will let her know" McPherson, *Battle Cry.*
"I have felt, ever since" McPherson, *Ordeal by Fire.*
"With malice toward none" Lincoln, *Speeches and Writings.*
"On reaching the door" Douglass, *Life and Times.*
"Here comes my friend" Douglass, *Life and Times.*
"Edward, unless you come" Channing, *Confederate Ordeal.*
"with empty stomachs" McCarthy, *Detailed Minutiae.*
"A note was handed" Botkin, *Civil War Treasury.*
"We were startled by heavy" Trudeau, *Men of War.*
"Richmond was literally a sea" Commanger, *Blue and the Gray.*
"Old men and women" Trudeau, *Men of War.*
"Thank God I have lived" McPherson, *Battle Cry.*
"I wonder if I could get" Foote, Civil War, *vol. 3.*
"There is nothing left for me" McPherson, *Ordeal by Fire.*
"In my rough traveling suit" Grant, Personal Memoirs.
"I have come to meet you" Commanger, *Blue and the Gray.*
"They fall on each other's" McPherson, *Ordeal by Fire.*
"The war is over" McPherson, *Battle Cry.*
"It is by miracles" Commanger, *Blue and the Gray.*
"That is the last speech" McPherson, *Battle Cry.*
"We must both be more" Carpenter, *Six Months.*
"I can't save him" Sandburg, *Abraham Lincoln.*
"Now he belongs to the ages." Sandburg, *Abraham Lincoln.*
"I am glad to see one real" McPherson, *Battle Cry.*
"We are all Americans." McPherson, *Battle Cry.*

What Ever Happened To . . .

"Useless, useless" Winik, *April 1865.*
"If I desired to kill the Senator" Schlesinger, *Congress Investigates.*
"Oh, I pitched in with them" Haskell, *Battle of Gettysburg.*
"Jeff Davis Captured in Hoop Skirts" Ross, *First Lady of the South.*
"Hello, I am Mrs. Grant" Ross, *First Lady of the South.*
"Forty years of my life" Douglass, *Life and Times.*
"God bless you, Douglas." Wells, *Stephen Douglas.*
"I am naturally fond of adventure" Edmonds, *Nurse and Spy.*
"We wish now for good feeling" Freeman, *R. E. Lee.*
"No, I will go right back" Freeman, *R. E. Lee.*
"There was a cheerless cold rain" Commanger, *Blue and the Gray.*
"I know this foul murder" Chesnut, *Diary from Dixie.*
"Now in this world" Oates, *Abraham Lincoln.*
"I feel that a great weight" McClellan, *McClellan's Own Story.*
"to place my side of the story" McClellan, *McClellan's Own Story.*
"It were better for his memory" Sears, *George B. McClellan.*
"[They] could hardly believe it was" Ransom, *Andersonville Diary.*
"I am sick and tired of fighting" Fellman, *Citizen Sherman.*
"So you're the little woman" Hedrick, *Harriet Beecher Stowe.*
"Save my civil rights bill." Sumner, *Works of Charles Sumner.*
"All they need is an equal" Uya, *Robert Smalls.*

Index

Steve Sheinkin

During many years spent writing American history textbooks, Steve Sheinkin filled fat files with all the amazing stories and surprising quotes that texbook editors would never let him use. Now he is finally using all that material to write history books that kids will actually want to read. He has also written *Which Way to the Wild West?*, which relates the breathtaking adventure of America's westward expansion, and *Two Miserable Presidents*, the amazing and terrible tale of the Civil War. Steve lives in Brooklyn, New York, with his wife and daughter.

Tim Robinson

Tim Robinson's work has graced the pages of many children's books and appears regularly in major newspapers and magazines. He lives in Croton-on-Hudson, New York, with his wife, Marguerite, and their two sons, Wyatt and Luke.